# ★★★ THE ★★★
# PATRIOT'S
# GUIDE
## — TO —
# TAKING
# AMERICA
# BACK

To Kyle

Charles K.

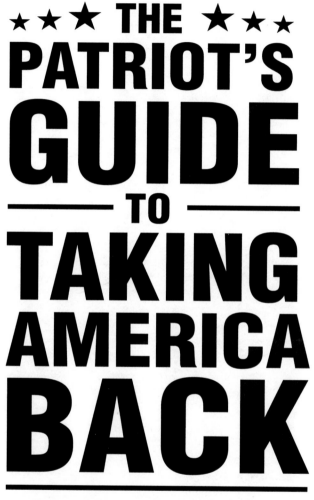

# ★★★ THE ★★★
# PATRIOT'S
# GUIDE
## —— TO ——
# TAKING
# AMERICA
# BACK

## CHARLES KRAUT

TATE PUBLISHING & Enterprises

Published by Tate Publishing & Enterprises, LLC
127 E. Trade Center Terrace | Mustang, Oklahoma 73064 USA
1.888.361.9473 | www.tatepublishing.com

Tate Publishing is committed to excellence in the publishing industry. The company reflects the philosophy established by the founders, based on Psalm 68:11,
*"The Lord gave the word and great was the company of those who published it."*

Published in the United States of America
ISBN: 978-1-61739-621-2
1. Polical Science, Constitutions
2. Political Science, Political Freedom & Security, General
10.11.09

# ★ ★ ★ DEDICATION ★ ★ ★

This book is dedicated to all who are willing to pledge their lives, their fortunes, and their sacred honor in defense of our liberty.

May this generation awaken from its slumber and restore those precious freedoms that were purchased at a heavy price.

How will you tell your children and your grandchildren what it *used* to be like to be free?

How will you explain that you let liberty just slip through your hands?

# TABLE OF CONTENTS

# INTRODUCTION

## The Greatest Crisis in American History

"Government is not reason; it is not eloquent; it is force. Like fire, it is a dangerous servant and a fearful master."

—George Washington

America today faces perhaps its greatest crisis, a "perfect storm" combining natural, economic, and political disasters and crises. Never in American history has our country had a greater need for educated, moral, and honest people to engage in the public debate and help our leaders shape America's domestic and foreign policies; at the same time, never in American history has our government been so completely dominated by self-proclaimed "elites" who wish to reshape America and the world into their own idea of utopia.

At the heart of these crises is the failure of the American people to support and defend their Constitution and maintain the government given to them by the Founding Fathers. This is not a recent failure but a cumulative one set in motion by men and women who either misunderstood the intentions of the Fathers or deliberately misconstrued them—or, in more recent times, ignored them altogether.

These crises include:

- Global warming
- The global economic recession/depression
- The War on Terror
- The War on Poverty
- The War on Drugs
- The decline of the dollar
- The accelerating slide of the American middle class into the lower class
- The massive growth of government and the resulting growth of debt
- The worldwide depletion of vital natural resources, and more

Most of these crises came about because we cast aside our Constitution and permitted greed, corruption, and the hunger for power to change us from free men and women into subjects of a powerful national government, a government incapable of governing itself—much less three hundred million Americans.

There are dozens of best-selling books about the problems America faces today. I call them "problem books," because every one I have read devotes most of its pages to the "problems" the author has discovered. Usually about half a dozen pages are devoted to the "solution," and in most cases the proposed solution is simply a laundry list of things the author thinks ought to be done. Seldom is any consideration given to the means by which these changes will be brought to pass. Such books may create public awareness, but they do little or nothing to effect a solution.

As you might expect, these "problems," whose exposition is so profitable to these authors, differ in their nature depending upon the authors' political philosophy. There are those who say that we have too little government, and those who say we have too much. There are those who say that our national debt is a huge problem and those who say that it is no problem at all. There are those who say that the emission of carbon dioxide by industry is causing global warming, while others can find no evidence to support that contention.

The problems discussed by most of these authors are complex. Some of them are not really "problems" but situations and artificial "crises" that politicians use as an excuse to act and seize power. It is almost impossible to stay on top of these issues and to determine for ourselves what is genuine and what is not. It is easy for people to become swayed by emotional appeals, particularly when they are ignorant of the facts. Our own personal experience colors the way we look at things.

This book is not a "problem" book. I will spend as little time as possible discussing problems, and when I do so, it will be to create awareness. The primary problem I will focus on is the shift America has made from its constitutional foundation to something more closely resembling a socialist welfare state, and the loss of personal freedom that has accompanied that shift. Many Americans are just now becoming aware that this is a serious problem. There are many others who are doing their best to force this shift upon us. Some of them are dedicated socialists or communists who have sworn to destroy the constitutional government of the United States. I would like to think that the rest of those who are moving us away from the Constitution are either misguided or simply have no appreciation of the value of freedom.

For these reasons, I am going to try to be very careful in describing the destruction of our freedom and the loss of our Constitution. I believe that these things are proceeding rapidly. The pace of change has accelerated in recent years. The American people are throwing away their liberty in exchange for the government's promises to take care of them. We are changing this country from a land of freedom to something much more totalitarian and authoritative. We have permitted the creation of a ruling class, an "elite" who consider themselves wiser and better than the rest of us, and who therefore are fit to rule.

If Americans had publicly and openly debated the shift from a constitutional republic to a welfare state, and had been adequately informed about those choices, I would be more willing to let things take their course, for the will of the people must be respected. Instead, these changes have been made over decades and have been brought about through deceit, hypocrisy, extortion, manipulation, fraud, and overstepping authority. The American people have been manipulated into certain beliefs and opinions by a constant stream of heavily biased opinion and by disinformation disguised as fact. We have been made to feel guilty about certain things and then made to believe that the only remedy to assuage our guilt is to recompense some supposedly aggrieved party or group or minority. This recompense becomes permanent, and we create large groups of people who benefit from our collective guilt.

The United States was founded on certain principles and ideals. Those principles and ideals have been cast aside and replaced by other, far less lofty notions. We once had the American Dream larger than life before us, and we responded by being larger than life. We were people of integrity, good moral character, and strong religious belief. We were involved in our communities, and we knew our neighbors. We had hope for the future because we knew that our hard work would be rewarded.

Decades ago, strident and persistent voices began to spring up to call us hypocrites and fools for being the kind of people we were. We were told that because we were a wealthy nation, there was no limit to what we could do. Many of us came to believe that we were exempt from the laws that had regulated other societies. We thought we had created something new, and we declared our independence from God and rejected the notions of commandments and obedience.

Over time, these voices were joined by many others, until today there are major industries devoted to the destruction of religion, morality, and even integrity in American life. Slowly, we began to believe that our most cherished values were indeed flawed. Rather than rushing toward the beliefs espoused by these new voices, however, a vacuum was created. Americans doubted their goodness and the rightness of the cause of freedom, but we have not fully accepted any substitutes for our values—not yet, at least.

We began to feel ashamed at our unwillingness to permit "choice" by allowing a pregnant woman to destroy the unborn child in her womb. We became convinced that our laws against immorality were prudish and Victorian. We were led to believe that we had an obligation to share our wealth with those less fortunate and that it was proper to take from those who *have* and give it to those who *have not.*

Those strident voices are still loud in our ears today, and yet they will not address the issues that have arisen because of the guilt and shame they created. Back then—fifty, sixty, seventy years ago—we were a nation of strong, loving, two-parent families. The statistics on immorality, divorce, broken homes, drug abuse, alcoholism, and crime were a tiny fraction of what they are today. As a nation we were better educated, more obedient, more homogeneous, and more desirous of making America a better place for our children and our grandchildren.

Today the prisons are full to overflowing, for the United States has incarcerated a higher percentage of its population than perhaps any other country in history. Our once cherished morals were replaced by "the new morality," which rapidly morphed into complete immorality. We fought a "War on Drugs" and suffered a terrible defeat. We permitted pornography to sweep across

America like a tidal wave of filth because the voices told us that if we didn't like it we didn't have to look at it.

The famous evangelist Billy Graham is said to have declared, "If God does not judge America, he will have to apologize to Sodom and Gomorrah." That's quite a condemnation of what we have allowed ourselves to become.

America has paid a terrible price for throwing itself off a cliff. Because our misbehavior has created such massive social problems, our government has gladly stepped in to take control of things we should have controlled ourselves.

In a few short years we changed from the nation of unlimited opportunity to a nation of dependents. Literacy and education began to plummet, while drug abuse, alcoholism, divorce, and immorality became terrible plagues that continue to devastate the landscape.

Think about how we are treated today by our government. Our government now provides services for which it has created a need. Our government expects us to indulge ourselves in our weaknesses and is pleased to pass more and more laws to try to control our conduct and build more and more prisons for the ever-increasing numbers of people who will not be controlled. Our government creates agencies and support groups and courts. Families that are deemed unable to care for themselves are broken up. Some of them become wards of the state. Our government does not expect its citizens to hold to any moral standards at all but instead has created the systems necessary to deal with the problems brought on by our immorality.

In this and in many other ways Americans are treated as subjects by our government. This is not the way it should be. Millions of Americans are angry and frustrated because of the changes that have taken place. There is no outlet for our anger except to vent it. There is no organization we can join in which we can convert our anger into useful effort that will help to remedy these problems.

This book is a plea for Americans to educate themselves, to regain their self-respect, and to become more obedient, more honest, and more moral so that we can see how very much we are about to lose. United we stand; divided we fall. There are deep divisions and minor cracks that separate us and keep us from working together. Apathy, ignorance, uninformed opinions, prejudice, avarice, greed, corruption—all these and more help pave the expressway to serfdom we are traveling today.

I am no political expert, nor do I claim to have any special knowledge about the problems facing us or the solutions. My expertise is in helping individuals to find purpose and meaning in their lives. Many Americans need a cause, a banner around which we can rally, an eternal flame we can stoke with our own energy and devotion. What greater cause can we serve than to defend the freedoms made available to us through the Constitution of the United States? You may answer, "Serving our God is a greater and higher purpose than serving our country," and you would be right. However, if you lived under the vast majority of governments in the history of our world you would not have had the freedom to worship God in your own way unless you chose the "state" religion.

Defending the Constitution is a righteous aim that requires the best in us. The cause of freedom includes defending the rights of all men to worship their God as they see fit. The Constitution is a solid foundation upon which men and women may build a better world.

## An Inspired Document

The Constitution is the greatest and most important political document in the history of mankind. It was put together by a group of men who, like all of us, had widely differing opinions about the proper role of government. That they produced our Constitution after lengthy debate and political wrangling is nothing short of a miracle.

Many people, this author included, believe the Constitution to be an inspired document. By that we mean that creating it required nothing less than divine intervention. The right people had to be brought together after having prepared themselves by years of study. They had to overcome personal feelings and preconceived notions to draft a unique document that would form the foundation of the greatest government in the world. Americans were given a great gift; unfortunately, we have not appreciated it nor labored to preserve it.

Having a constitution enables Americans to enjoy a degree of freedom seldom found in human history. It restricts government in order to preserve individual freedom. It encourages us to act within it so that we may lead happy and prosperous lives. Much of the credit for the great American miracle of economic growth can be given to the Constitution; the rest can be given to the initiative of Americans and the immense natural resources we have found and exploited here. America should be the greatest country in the world because it has the greatest government. It is not because we have discarded the Constitution.

Americans should learn the Constitution as children, memorizing it along with other key documents of freedom. All of us should cherish this great document and strive each day to be the moral and upright people it requires. We do not.

Since the day of its ratification the Constitution has been under attack by those who have a different view of how men should be governed. Over the decades, as the transition to a national government and then to a welfare state accelerated, the attacks have become more powerful and dangerous. Those today who would destroy the Constitution have their own agendas and are unwilling to allow all men and women the freedom to create their own destiny. Rather, they wish to institute means by which they will obtain power for themselves by convincing us that what they have to offer is better. What they offer usually can be summed up in two words: *wealth redistribution.* If the central government can convince people that they can rob the public treasury for their own gain, they will abandon the Constitution and willingly enslave themselves. This is what we have done. To prevent such a thing from happening, the Founding Fathers wisely added the Tenth Amendment to the Bill of Rights:

"The powers not delegated to the United States by the Constitution, nor prohibited by it to the States, are reserved to the States respectively, or to the people."

The Framers wanted to ensure that the new federal government would have more power than it did under the Articles of Confederation but not enough to become all-powerful. For this reason the Tenth Amendment was added shortly after the ratification of the Constitution. It ensures that all powers not specifically granted to the federal government are reserved to the states or to the people.

For many years, even prior to the Civil War, the Tenth Amendment has been largely ignored by our federal government. Governments always usurp power, and the Tenth Amendment has been successfully attacked by those in Washington. It became easier to do so when Chief Justice John Marshall instituted the concept of judicial review, and the notion that the affairs of each state would be subject to the rulings of the Supreme Court. In addition, because the federal government alone is empowered by the Constitution to coin or borrow money, it had a powerful tool in seizing power from the states and from the people. Truly, the power to tax is the power to destroy, and the federal government has used and expanded that power both to increase its control over the lives of Americans and to manipulate governments at all levels through compulsion and mandates.

Initially the new nation was divided between the Federalists and those who believed in states' rights. An Anti-Federalist party had been established in an effort to prevent the ratification of the Constitution and the Bill of Rights, but that party ceased to exist after the ratification. Between 1792 and 1824 the two national political parties were the Federalist Party, founded by Alexander Hamilton, and the Democratic-Republican party founded by Thomas Jefferson and James Madison. There were sharp divisions between them on the issues of a strong central government versus states' rights. Because the newly formed

United States faced many challenges domestically and abroad, the actions of the early Presidents and Congresses, along with those of the fledgling Supreme Court, established traditions and interpretations of the Constitution that carry through to our day.

As a Federalist and one of the authors of *The Federalist Papers,* Alexander Hamilton pleaded for a central bank. At first his efforts were rebuffed, but the United States subsequently made three attempts at central banking, including our current Federal Reserve Bank. The first was a dismal failure. The second was suppressed by President Andrew Jackson despite evidence that it was performing a vital function. The third, our current Federal Reserve, has used the concept of a national bank to take upon itself immense power. It has abused its power and almost destroyed our currency.

Along with a central bank, many other ideas of the Federalists were put into practice at one time or another, and their cumulative effect has been to strengthen Washington at the expense of all other levels of government. Today we have a *national* government rather than a *federal* government, contrary to all the wishes and intentions of the Founding Fathers. This national government extends into every aspect of life and subjects us to countless laws and regulations, all of which have created a nation far different than a constitutional republic. Americans are far less free under this national government than we were under the Constitution.

John Adams said:

> "Remember, democracy never lasts long. It soon wastes, exhausts, and murders itself. There never was a democracy yet that did not commit suicide."

The history of constitutional republics is quite similar to that of democracies. Republics often disintegrate or are forced into dictatorships. Few have lasted more than two hundred years. There is one significant exception in world history, however.

# The Oldest Government in the World Today

The Isle of Man is a small island in the Irish Sea between Ireland and northern England. The country has a Parliament whose activities date back to the Viking settlements, which began in the eighth century of the first millennium a.d. No other parliament in the world has such a long, unbroken record. It is instructive to see what the people of the Isle of Man do today to preserve the longest-running parliamentary government in human history.

July 5 is the Manx National Day. On that date each year, a ceremony has taken place that has continued unchanged except in detail for more than one thousand years. This ceremony at the ancient site of Tynwald is rich both in tradition and history. As much as anything else it is a Christian religious service, one in which the hand of God is acknowledged in enabling and defending the prosperity and freedom of the Manx people.

What might America be like today if hundreds of thousands of Americans would gather to Washington on a specific day each year to acknowledge and give thanks for God's blessings and to perform penitence and ask His forgiveness?

Manx National Day is the day on which all proposed laws that have been approved by the legislature are promulgated and ratified. On many occasions the entire body of laws created over the previous twelve months has been read to the assembled multitude, and at times the entire Constitution has been read as well. All the proceedings are performed both in English and in Manx, the ancient native language of the people of the Isle of Man.

The inhabitants of the Isle of Man are encouraged to take an active role in learning and understanding the laws which govern them and in teaching them to their children. There is much to be said for tradition, and to maintain a way of life which carries with it significant social mores and the expectation that each citizen will be a responsible citizen.

The people of the Isle of Man have not given into materialism, neither have they removed God from their public or private life. Their government has served them well, and continues to do so today. One thousand years of history brings many changes, but tradition and shared beliefs have held the Isle of Man together longer than any other government in the history of the world.

## America is Not the Isle of Man

Though this example is instructive, it is by no means perfectly applicable to our situation here in the United States. This country is home to far more people than the Isle of Man, and the larger the population the easier it is for the government to become corrupt. America was not founded specifically as a Christian nation but rather one in which some of the principles of Christianity were enshrined.

America is a land of tremendous natural resources, which has given rise to the creation of tremendous fortunes and a growing spread from the top economic strata to the bottom. However, one trend clearly separates us from the Isle of Man. In my lifetime, I have seen a dramatic shift away from traditional belief and culture and behavior toward a far more casual style of living unfettered by social mores, morality, and religious belief. This transition has been accompanied by a change in American culture from a true melting pot, where immigrants are anxious to learn to speak English and become assimilated into our society, to today's world where we claim to celebrate diversity and encourage people to hold onto their language, their culture, and their own standards. Both trends seem to be destructive of our constitutional liberties.

## Power Tends to Corrupt

"Power tends to corrupt, and absolute power corrupts absolutely. Great men are almost always bad men.'
    –John Emerick Edward Dahlberg Acton,
    known simply as Lord Acton (1834–1902)

It is axiomatic that when given a little authority most people will follow their natural inclination to seek more power. The more power one has, the more one wants. Power corrupts whatever it touches, and government in the hands of the power-hungry changes from the servant of the people to its master. However, most people today have no idea how intensely and completely power corrupts. It is even more so when those who are in power surround themselves with sycophants and admirers, who are publicly applauded everywhere they go as if they were something special. The rise of the "personality cult" is not restricted to Third World nations and banana republics; the concept infects every nation throughout the world, as it always has.

The American people have forgotten what the Constitution is all about. More accurately, they never knew. Few public schools teach the Constitution today. Many law schools teach only twentieth century interpretations of the Constitution rather than the Constitution itself. Generations now living have been taught that we have Constitutional rights—and have expanded that list of "rights" far beyond anything contained in the Constitution or envisioned by the Founding Fathers.

For example, our current administration in Washington is telling us that health care is a *right*. The Constitution is explicit about our rights as free men and women; we have the right to pursue life, liberty, and happiness secure from government intrusion as long as we adhere to the Constitution and live in integrity and morality. Beyond that, life is a risk—which is as it should be.

The Constitution establishes a framework of law unlike any other, for it grants American citizens the opportunity to pursue their dreams in ways often proscribed under other systems. The Constitution works because it does not grant us rights; instead, it acknowledges that all men possess natural and inalienable rights, and that government must be restrained in its efforts to take those rights away.

# The Right to Succeed or Fail

As Americans living under the Constitution, we have the right to succeed or fail. If we fail, we may find a charitable organization or individual willing to "grubstake" us to another chance. Under no circumstances may a Constitutional government "grubstake" or bail out its citizens, for doing so is a means of redistributing wealth. That is socialism, and socialism is as far opposed to republican, constitutional government as it could possibly be.

Under socialism, property rights are stripped away. Without the profit motive and the incentive of owning the fruits of your own labor, people under socialism or communism lose the desire to produce and pay their own way. Life has no purpose when one cannot improve his or her own circumstances outside of becoming a party apparatchik.

Under socialism everyone has free health care, guaranteed employment, and "cradle to grave" support. Unfortunately, because this Utopian concept removes the incentive to produce, socialism quickly fails because not enough is produced. As Walt Kelly famously put it, "The shortages will be divided among the peasants." America should have learned its lesson well by witnessing what went on in Communist China and the Soviet bloc during the Cold War. We didn't, perhaps because we were being lulled into complacency by the many voices proclaiming that "America is rich. America can afford to be generous. America can share its blessings with the poor. America lifts its lamp beside the golden door, inviting in the poor, the homeless, the refugees."

This siren song was believed by many, starting with Franklin D. Roosevelt, who decided to become America's first truly Socialist president and redistribute wealth at a frightening rate. Unfortunately, he only managed to prolong and deepen the worst financial crisis in history and almost bankrupted America in the process. Though his programs had popular support, they were economically unsustainable and ineffective. These programs also created a "social safety net," which made millions of Americans dependent upon their government.

We didn't learn from the experience of the New Deal but went on from one administration to the next, creating more and more rights for more and more special interest groups. We couldn't stop at our border either; we decided we were smart enough to go into other nations—by force if they resisted our peaceful overtures—and remake their governments in the image of what ours used to be. We invited millions of aliens into the United States (or looked the other way when they snuck across the border) and provided them all the benefits available to citizens (and more) because we were so rich and powerful we could best express our wonderfulness through our magnanimity.

It's amazing what you can do when you are generous with other people's money—and when you have the power to take money from those who have it.

This is America today - a once-great and wealthy nation that has squandered its wealth in foolish and wasteful spending dedicated to keeping our elected officials in office and granting them more and more power. We have been told that the Constitution is no longer relevant, for it does not address the critical issues of our day; we have transcended it in order to better care for our citizens. The next logical step, they say, is to scrap the Constitution in favor of something more "relevant" to the forced transfer of wealth and the seemingly irreversible march toward socialism.

There is one great problem with this. Even if wealth redistribution was permitted by the Constitution, no country can afford to maintain socialism for long. As people discover they can get benefits from the government, they lose their incentive to produce. Soon (as in today) there are more recipients of government benefits than there are taxpayers to pay for them. Such a government bankrupts itself through supposedly good intentions and unintended consequences.

How do elected officials escape these unintended consequences? Why are they not held responsible for the violation of their oath of office, their failure to support and defend the Constitution, and the deliberate bankrupting of the country to promote their own selfish agenda?

Elected officials portray themselves as the saviors of the people. When their foolish schemes go awry, as they almost always do, they claim that outside influences beyond their control caused the program to fail. All that is required, they tell us, is to expand the program and throw more money at it, and everything will be fine. In this way they always position themselves as "fighting the good fight."

Win or lose, they make themselves look like heroes. You can hear them every day on NPR, weeping and wailing about how sad it is that Americans are too selfish to permit a property tax to be raised by just one penny in order to permit an underprivileged child to play a varsity sport. Such appeals are very persuasive, for they seem to be promoting a common good while elevating the underprivileged. All they are really doing is attempting to steal more money from taxpayers so that they may redistribute it to people who will re-elect them. This is institutionalized compassion at its worst, for it makes the overstressed taxpayers appear selfish and mean—as it is intended to do.

## Changing the Subject

Elected officials are also very experienced at changing the subject. When their bad ideas backfire, they find an unrelated issue they can utilize to dominate the media. For example, when President Clinton was embroiled in the Monica Lewinsky scandal, he found it convenient to conduct a military attack against a pharmaceutical plant in Sudan. The move was entirely unexpected, and it seems to have had the desired effect. When the facts came to light, and it was discovered that the building was indeed a legitimate pharmaceutical plant, the story quickly disappeared.

Today, changing the subject has been elevated to an art form. Americans are kept off balance by a constant barrage of stories that capture our attention, whether for a moment or a month, and distract us from the really important issues. It's almost like the "bread and circuses" of ancient Rome, when the people were fed, entertained, and isolated from what was really going on in the Empire, to the extent that the Emperor and the entire government left Rome, and the city forever lost its relevance. It did not lose its welfare benefits, however.

National healthcare is a "change the subject" issue. The "healthcare crisis" is a fabrication and a lie. As is the case with global warming, the advocates of national healthcare use fuzzy math, incorrect statistics, statements taken out of context, and worthless and misleading information to keep their issue on the front page of every newspaper across the country, while the really pressing issues of the day are being downplayed and ignored.

National healthcare may be little more than a smokescreen for the other activities of Congress and the president in dealing with the economic crisis by heavily favoring Wall Street and the unions. The bankrupting of the United States proceeds apace, while Congress tries to spend as much money as it possibly can on worthless programs that will do nothing to pull the United States out of its depression. Their efforts are roughly equivalent to straightening the deck chairs on the Titanic after it struck the iceberg.

As to why elected officials are not held to their oath of office I can only speculate. The most likely reason is that the few remaining Americans who understand the Constitution have no voice at all in government or in the media. Ron Paul is a lone voice in the House of Representatives, and the media tend to marginalize and suppress his ideas.

## The Constitution is on Life Support

Our inspired Constitution is on life support, and our elected officials are calling for Dr. Kevorkian. If Americans do not rise up immediately in great numbers and raise the banner of freedom, we will lose our Constitution and the last hope our world has for freedom.

# Rolling a Snowball

This book is my attempt to figuratively stand on a snow-covered hill and make a snowball, which I hope will grow massively as it rolls downhill. The "snowball" is the love of freedom, and it will grow only if that love can be planted in the hearts of millions of Americans. In the pages that follow I will discuss a few of the many threats to our freedom and what I believe we must do now if we are to have any hope of restoring America to its constitutional foundation.

When I began working on this book, my intent was to help the various and numerous "protest" groups I belong to like the Tea Party Patriots and the Campaign for Liberty find their footing and organize themselves into an effective force advocating a return to a constitutional republic. It didn't take long to learn that the national laws regarding such organizations (they are listed as 501c(4) organizations) prevent them from doing what they must be able to do. Instead, the advantage is entirely with the special interest groups who can solicit funds at will and are permitted access to the halls of power. They are free, it seems, to campaign for candidates as they see fit.

Based on my understanding of our current laws regarding political organizations established as 501(c)(4)s for tax purposes, laws which are patently unfair and contrary to the spirit and intent of the Constitution, the only way to effectively advocate a return to the Constitution is through a political party. For reasons you will discover in Chapter Sixteen, only one political party today has the ability to accomplish this. That party already exists, and is known in most states as the Constitution Party. This party has as its platform the Constitution itself and certain principles derived from it and other documents pertaining to the founding of the United States. The Constitution Party has labored in obscurity for too long. It is time for it to become known by all Americans as the *only* party dedicated to the Constitution, a document we must respect, understand, and defend.

Please join me and decide for yourself whether you would like to be part of the struggle for freedom. Millions are needed, and all are welcome. Please leave behind any belief you may have that the government owes you a living. Your freedoms—and those of your children and grandchildren—are in your hands.

—Lexington, Virginia
March 2010

# OVERVIEW

"My God! How little do my country men know what precious blessings they are in possession of, and which no other people on earth enjoy."

—Thomas Jefferson, 1785

"The greatest dangers to liberty lurk in insidious encroachment by men of zeal, well-meaning but without understanding."

—Louis D. Brandeis

There are some in this once-great country who understand and respect the principles and designs of our great Constitution. For the most part, their voices are not heard nor recognized, particularly in the halls of power.

You are holding in your hands a blueprint for a project that will restore our Republic to its constitutional foundation. As you will see in the chapters that follow, making that restoration happen will require that people act against human nature. Many will have to set aside personal opinions, beliefs, and ideas. Those who hold political office will need to be educated about the very Constitution they have taken an oath to defend and preserve, for most of them know little or nothing about it.

The United States in 2010 is similar to the Thirteen Colonies in 1776 in one important aspect. In 1776 many of the colonists favored the Crown and did not support an uprising against the authority of the king. Today, many Americans oppose a return to constitutional principles, for they interpret the Constitution differently than those who framed it.

Other Americans will remain on the sidelines, happy to receive their living from the labors of others for as long as they can. Finally, those who will engage and bring about this great work are a minority who love freedom and believe in moral and ethical conduct.

In 1776 the majority of those living in the Thirteen Colonies were either loyal to the British Crown or declared themselves neutral in the coming conflict. That conflict would bring about a new birth of freedom in what would become these United States. There may have been as many as a third of the colonists who supported and sustained the ideas of freedom and self-government, but they were clearly a minority. The Colonists brought about a miracle as they overcame one of the world's greatest military and naval forces, and then produced a truly inspired document by which the people of this country would be governed. All of this was accomplished despite overwhelming odds.

The odds are just as great in our day. Fully 47 percent of those living in the United States pay no income taxes. Millions receive benefits from numerous governmental handout programs. Since they are unconcerned about paying for the benefits they receive they vote for whoever promises to continue and increase their benefits. Today both the Democrats and Republicans have been forced to pander to them if they wish to win elections. We may have already passed the point of no return on the road to socialism.

Another large minority believes that America's greatness comes from its compassion and that our government has an obligation to play the role of Robin Hood—to rob the rich to help the poor. This notion is completely unconstitutional, but it has become conventional wisdom. Because this incorrect doctrine has become the conventional wisdom, we no longer question the validity of these wealth transfer programs; we only debate how much to take from the taxpayers and give to others. We also debate how much money we can print and spend without collapsing the dollar.

The colonists who were willing to give their all in the cause of freedom had a "secret weapon." True, they had faith in divine Providence. They were men and women of integrity and sound character, and they were visionary in seeing what this land could become. The most important thing they possessed was their love of freedom. They wanted to throw off the shackles of tyranny and free themselves from serfdom. They wanted to live in a land where their own efforts would be rewarded, where their opportunities were limited only by their own abilities. Their "secret weapon" was their belief that men could govern themselves, and that no man had a God-given right to rule over them.

The oppressive policies and taxes of England's King George III literally forced the colonists into declaring their independence—and then into open rebellion against his authority because he treated the colonists as subjects. Our own government today treats taxpayers as subjects. Taxpayers provide the money with which politicians buy votes. We have reached the point where if we do not throw off the shackles imposed upon us by our government in Washington, those of us who work will become slaves to those who will not.

We only need to look at the taxes we pay. In 2009 the average American worked from January 1 through April 16 just to pay his taxes. In other words, every penny that you and I made for those first three and half months of the year went to government, at some level, in what is called a "forced exaction." If we calculate the amount of deficit spending conducted by our federal government in the years leading up to 2009 and assume that we will pay it off year by year as well, we need to work for the government well into August.

If we then calculate the costs of the stimulus packages and enormous deficits being incurred by our federal government in the Obama Administration, we suddenly discover that we could work for the government all year long and have nothing left to live on. What better opportunity could we have to take back our government from those we have elected and sent to Washington?

## Principles and Integrity

"To compel a man to subsidize with his taxes the propagation of ideas which he disbelieves and abhors is sinful and tyrannical."

—Thomas Jefferson

In this book I speak of principles because I must. We cannot be bystanders watching the destruction of freedom, nor can we merely be vocal critics of our elected officials. We must stand for something of value and show all men why it is of such great value. This is a delicate work, for freedom cannot be forced upon anyone. Millions of Americans are happy to be enslaved by government as long as they are feeding from the public trough; convincing them to wean themselves away from those handouts is an all but impossible task.

It is unreasonable to believe that a majority of Americans will ever fully devote themselves to the cause of freedom. This complicates our task, for if we are to return America to its constitutional foundation, most, if not all, of the handout programs enacted by the United States government must be stopped. Our success will depend upon establishing an influential political force for good. We cannot simply expect to replace the entire Congress and the president with people who thoroughly understand and love the Constitution; we will always have to work with those on the opposite side of the fence. It may seem ironic that people who have neither belief nor interest in the Constitution have sworn a solemn oath to sustain and defend it, but life is full of ironies. Our task will be to "hold their feet to the fire" and make sure that the American people know when their actions and their proposals violate both the Constitution and common sense.

Once enough Americans understand and respect the Constitution and realize how much harm our elected officials have done, they may begin to take the necessary steps to dismantle the welfare state. Many people today maintain the vain hope that we can have both "guns and butter," meaning that we can pay for programs mandated by the Constitution such as national defense as well as the social safety net programs of the welfare state. This is not the case.

Americans have very little education in either the Constitution or basic economics. We have allowed ourselves to believe that the government can indeed provide us with a comfortable living, though we have no idea where the money will come from. We have not reached the point where we will demand that our elected officials stop spending money we don't have or face recall. We must get to that point. It is simply not enough to trust our elected officials to know any more about economics than we do, particularly because their motivations are political and they hold the power to tax and spend.

Deficit spending and the creation of an enormous national debt are just one of the ways in which our government has failed in their responsibilities, but it is a very important one. The emergence of the United States after World War II as a "superpower" placed the U.S. dollar in a position of predominance over all other currencies. Unfortunately, this freed Congress and the president to squander the trust and respect the world placed in us and our money. As a result, the United States has become the world's greatest debtor, and our once mighty U.S. dollar is in rapid decline as people and governments all over the world realize that its value will never again be sustained by the government that issues it.

Our Federal Reserve, a nominally private organization created by an act of Congress, wants us to believe that there is no limit to the number of dollars we can create and spend; however, there are very real limits. It will be very painful when we fund ourselves up against them.

The point here is that elected officials and appointed judges have a moral and ethical obligation not only to uphold and defend the Constitution of the United States; they must also act in such a way as to support the principles and ideals on which our country was founded. That point was lost many years ago, probably sometime between World War II and the commencement of the Korean War, as Americans faced dangers and problems no nation had ever faced.

## Government by Crisis

"I predict future happiness for Americans if they can prevent the government from wasting the labors of the people under the pretense of taking care of them."

—Thomas Jefferson

Our federal government has learned a valuable lesson from the pages of history. Power can be seized during times of crisis, and governments always want more power. The September 11 attacks are a classic instance of government taking advantage of a crisis. In an amazingly short period of time after the attacks Congress passed and the president signed the USA Patriot Act—one of the worst pieces of legislation ever passed by any government. Our government played upon our fears of terrorism and promised to keep us safe if we would just surrender what turned out to be a large chunk of our freedom. The Patriot Act opened the door to numerous crimes against the Constitution, including:

- The arrest without indictment or trial of American citizens,

- The granting of eavesdropping authority without benefit of warrant on numerous police and investigative agencies,

- The seizure of assets held by private citizens without legal recourse,

- The requirement that financial institutions make the personal records of all of their customers available to government snoops, and much more.

Our federal government has learned the lesson so well that it is now engaged in creating and inventing crises so that it may step in and seize more power. As I mentioned before, national health care is one such instance; "cap and trade" is another. Both major political parties have demonstrated a great willingness to go along with this, which is why I have little hope that either party will ever again deserve the trust and respect of those who love the Constitution.

In Part One of *The Patriot's Guide* we will discuss freedom and the love of freedom. I will share a frightening vision of a future which is all too near to our present condition. In Part Two we will talk about where we are as a nation in 2010 and how our federal government has become very corrupt. In Part Three we will engage in a thought experiment about what our country might look like today if we had held fast to the principles embodied in the Constitution, and what would need to be done if we were to return to it.

Finally, in Part Four I will share my ideas about an organization, most likely a political party because of the laws regarding political activism on the books today, which will have the best chance of moving us back to our constitutional foundation. This is the heart of the book. My recommendations will be detailed and thorough, taking advantage of my experience in working with people and in training leaders. You will have your own ideas about how to do these things, but I urge you to test out my recommendations as precisely as possible.

I cannot see any other way to restore the Constitution in today's highly polarized environment unless these recommendations are implemented. Of course, where my recommendations violate laws either currently in effect or which will be passed into law at some future date, I will need to change my approach. For this reason I have solicited comments from people who know far more about political activism and political organizations than I do. I solicit your comments and ideas, for this is obviously a "work in progress" that deserves to be improved constantly.

You will notice several quotes from Thomas Jefferson in this book. Jefferson, the author of the Declaration of Independence and our third president, was a Virginian, one of eight presidents to come from that state. Though Jefferson supported the idea of replacing the Articles of Confederation with something better suited to a growing nation, he was always cautious of allowing government to gain too much power. He was frequently at odds with Alexander Hamilton and John Adams, both strong Federalists. Jefferson lost every battle he fought with John Marshall, fourth chief justice of the Supreme Court and likewise a strong Federalist. It is ironic that during the administration of the one president who most embodied the principle of state's rights, the federal government implemented sweeping initiatives to increase its power at the expense of the people and the states.

It is incumbent upon those of us who love freedom to re-establish the Constitution of these United States as the supreme law of the land. I have no doubt that we can accomplish this. Today Americans may not have the will to do so, but if we educate ourselves so that we may appreciate the blessings of freedom, we can become a free people once again.

# Part One

## Freedom

"Here is my advice as we begin the century that will lead to 2081. First, guard the freedom of ideas at all costs. Be alert that dictators have always played on the natural human tendency to blame others and to oversimplify. And don't regard yourself as a guardian of freedom unless you respect and preserve the rights of people you disagree with to free, public, unhampered expression."

—Gerard K. O'Neill, 2081

## CHAPTER ONE

# Do You Love Freedom?

We have enjoyed so much freedom for so long that we are perhaps in danger of forgetting how much blood it cost to establish the Bill of Rights.

—Felix Frankfurter

The Founding Fathers knew that they were establishing a new and untested government. The Declaration of Independence was a bold gesture, and when it was sent to King George it probably seemed very unlikely that it would stand. After all, England had the world's mightiest navy and a very powerful army and seemed almost invincible. It is difficult to comprehend the courage and faith of those who put their names to that sacred document in the hope that through their efforts a new birth of freedom might take place. History reminds us that many of them never recovered from the sacrifices they made because of their dedication to a principle.

The Founding Fathers knew, and attested in their writings, that the Republic which was created with the framing and ratification of the Constitution would require for its citizens people of integrity and morality, people who were willing to work to create their own destiny rather than having a destiny dictated to them by an autocrat.

Our America is very different from what the Founding Fathers envisioned. Americans today enjoy far less freedom than even the generation that preceded us. It seems as if each generation from the time of the ratification has found ways to restrict its freedoms in exchange for alien philosophies and ideologies, which have failed wherever they have been practiced.

In our day there are many who criticize our economic system as well as our government. Many of them feel that it is the responsibility of government to provide for the needs of the people in one way or another. Having government provide for any of the needs of its people beyond the common defense is a very dangerous thing, for the price exacted by government is always a portion of our freedom.

The dangers our republic faces today are numerous and grave. The majority of Americans are willing to sacrifice their freedom for a "mess of pottage." Politicians and judges have been more than willing to give Americans what they claimed they wanted, for in so doing those same politicians and judges have taken upon themselves more power and more control. Though we pride ourselves on having no king, we have allowed an elite class to be created, a class of people who believe themselves better than others and in many cases above the law.

This is very similar to what happens in totalitarian societies. At its peak the Soviet Union was governed by only eight million Communist Party members in a country of more than 200 million. As George Orwell stated in his book *Animal Farm,* this privileged party was like those pigs who were "more equal than others." A royal lineage, the ability to sway the mobs, the seizure of power by force, the persuasion of others to join our cause through the use of bribery, illegal maneuverings and tricks used to entrap the innocent—all these and more have been used by individuals and groups to gain and assert power over their fellow men.

It seems that human nature being what it is, men and women are inclined to seek their own good first and, for many, to the exclusion of all other things. Greed and the thirst for power are highly corrosive and lead people to do things that will harm others. It is perhaps surprising that any religion that teaches us to love our enemies and do good to those that the spitefully use us would have any success at all in a world dominated by those who seek power and privilege.

Clearly, the odds were against a group of men, empowered by their respective states to amend the federal government, to rise above self-interest in order to create something the world had never seen. The framers of the Constitution had never known anything but monarchy except through their education. Still, they managed to put together a document that could, if followed rigorously, create a nation in which no man would be master. The idea of sovereignty of the individual is a remarkable one that had seldom found expression in all of human history. The creation of a federal government, which would be subordinate to the people it governs and to the sovereign states within the union, was likewise a stroke of inspiration. No such thing had ever before existed in a form where strict limitations were placed upon the federal government.

Americans were given a priceless gift; the opportunity to throw off the shackles of kings, dictators, and debt and live their own lives as they saw fit. Americans were free to pursue education, a trade of their choice, the place where they would live and raise their families, the management of their government at all levels, and a very high degree of personal autonomy.

With this priceless gift came important responsibilities. Freedom is never free; responsible citizenship is a burden that must not be shifted to another. The Founding Fathers envisioned a nation of people who would seek learning in the science of government and actively participate in the political process in order to make America stronger and freer throughout its generations. Instead, they got the two-party system, a system better suited for herding sheep than for governing free men.

From the moment of its ratification Americans began to destroy their Constitution. Most of them simply went about their business and did not actively involve themselves in the political process. If they felt any particular gratitude toward the Founding Fathers, it was merely that under the Constitution they didn't have to submit themselves to the whims of a powerful government. We had opportunities to strengthen and improve the Constitution, but for the most part we did not.

We allowed the Supreme Court, for example, to assert itself far beyond the intent of the framers of the Constitution, with the result that today there are unelected judges at many levels who have taken to themselves the power not only to rule within their jurisdiction but also to "legislate from the bench" and dictate their personal standards and prerogatives to those they were appointed to serve. As has been the case with power-hungry men and women throughout all the ages of history, Americans who have been placed in positions of power have changed the Constitution and our country to suit their own personal tastes and ideas.

The point is that Americans allowed these things to happen basically because we couldn't be bothered. We had a continent to conquer, tremendous natural resources to plunder, an environment of stunning beauty to lay waste, and riches on every hand just for the taking. As long as the government didn't get in our way, why should we concern ourselves with what our leaders were doing?

The American people are like the frog in the frying pan. The heat has risen slowly so that we never realized we were being boiled to death. Our leaders took advantage of crises as wonderful opportunities to reshape the political landscape and to seize more power for themselves. We allowed Abraham Lincoln to write some of the earliest Executive Orders, justifying them because we were in a national emergency without precedent. More than 13,500 equally unconstitutional Executive Orders later, it's a little late to begin wondering how our constitutional provision of checks and balances was completely subverted.

Let's get back to the original question: Do you love freedom? This is what each of us needs to ask ourselves. It's a broad and sweeping question with many components. It is easy to say that we love freedom even though we have no intention of doing anything to preserve it. Do you love freedom enough to defend it? What sacrifices are you willing to make to ensure that your government serves you and not the other way around? Where will you draw the "line in the sand" and say to your elected officials "no more"?

The list of powers and authorities our government has taken upon itself, which are specifically not found in the Constitution, is very long—and becoming much longer. Our government has momentum. Just like a speeding freight train, it is very difficult to stop. Decades and even centuries of tradition of working around the Constitution have done tremendous damage to that document. To date, the American people have allowed all of these things to happen. Yes, there were protests and rebellion, but government found a way to suppress the former and crush the latter. It is a fearful thing to contemplate standing up against our all-powerful central government today, for it has created resources, which we as taxpayers have paid for, which can strip us of our freedom and our property without legal recourse. In many ways we face the same threat today from our government as the Colonists did from King George. Do you love freedom enough to make yourself a target of a powerful and abusive government?

Let's ask the question in a slightly different way. If you knew that 100 million Americans would stand with you in your fight to restore our constitutional freedoms and government, would that make you comfortable enough to get involved?

What if it were only 10 million Americans? Would you be less comfortable when such a (relatively) small number stood with you?

What if it were only 1 million Americans? Would you question your sanity in getting involved with a group that might be perceived as having no hope of effecting positive change?

What we're getting to is the question that many Americans must ask themselves now. We cannot afford to wait for 100 million Americans to get involved, because the other 99,000,000 are thinking the same thing. Do you have the courage to take a stand even if you are the only one doing so and could only hope that you would be able to recruit others to stand with you?

The Founding Fathers did. By signing the Declaration of Independence they knew they were putting all they had on the altar, and that in all likelihood they would stand alone when they were tried for treason against their king. They knew that there were many in the Thirteen Colonies who opposed them and who desired to remain loyal to King George. There were also a great many who, out of fear or for some other reason, chose not to get involved.

Our situation is no different. It is not a light thing that we ask Americans to learn to love freedom and to make sacrifices in its defense. Like the signers of the Declaration of Independence, we have little hope of success, because the odds are heavily against us. Prudence and wisdom might whisper to us that we are wasting our time and endangering all that we have worked for. Therefore, we must elevate this discussion one more level. Think about what you will leave behind when your mortal life is over. Do you love your children and your grandchildren and those yet unborn who will call you their ancestor enough to make the blessings of freedom available to them?

Americans are busy people. We occupy our lives with things that are important to us and things that are required of us. We are required, for example, to provide for ourselves and our families. We are forced to comply with the dictates of many different governments, all of which impose burdens upon us. Often what is important to us must be set aside so that we may meet the demands placed upon us. We commute an hour each way just to keep our job; we struggle to meet a monthly mortgage payment and all of our other financial obligations; we try to maintain our home and our possessions, and we watch helplessly as our government grabs more power and authority over us—even as it extracts more money from our wallets.

There is often little time to do things that we enjoy, things that we feel are very important and even things that we are passionate about. Perhaps no age in history has required the high level of education we must possess in order to be responsible citizens, but at the same time we are watching a wave of illiteracy and ignorance sweep across the country. There was a time, not so very long ago, when every school child would memorize significant portions, if not the entire text, of the Constitution, the Declaration of Independence, the Gettysburg address, and other famous documents.

We went to public school to learn and to be taught, not to gain self-esteem and be shown where to find information should we ever happen to need it. Histroically, military service has produced veterans who appreciate the blessings of freedom, but our generation has fewer veterans than many others. Today, millions of Americans cannot recite the Preamble to the Constitution from memory, find the United States on a map of the world, recognize the tune of our national anthem, or even speak English, perhaps the most important language in the entire world.

It is true that an uneducated populace is the more easily enslaved. It is true that people whose existence depends upon government handouts are likely to vote for more handouts. It is true that the entertainment media have a powerful influence over our thoughts and our beliefs. It is also true that the majority of what people hear today from all sources encourages them to spend money whether they have it or not, to do things for themselves because they "deserve it," to live for today, to game the system, to take advantage of everything the government is willing to give to us, and to sit back and trust others into whose hands we have placed our future and our children's future.

My response to all this is a simple one. For many years I have watched people grow and learn as they were asked to serve. When they accepted an assignment and prepared themselves to fulfill it they gained new talents and abilities of which they had been unaware. As they gained experience in fulfilling their assignment their confidence increased along with their ability to interact with others.

I believe that Americans will respond favorably and in great numbers to the call of freedom. Americans are not bad people; most of us are just not involved in good causes. As we invite them to participate in something of great value, they will accept the challenge and lift themselves. I believe that many tens of thousands will change their lives as they begin to recognize for the first time what it means to be a citizen of this great country.

This is why it is so vitally important that we begin *now* to educate the American people regarding the blessings of freedom and our divinely inspired Constitution. Give them an opportunity and a working knowledge of true principles, and they can accomplish anything.

We *can* take America back.

Freedom is ours to lose.

We dare not fail.

## CHAPTER TWO

# What Is Freedom?

Freedom may be more easily defined by what it *is not* than by what it *is*. Freedom has been the topic of endless debate over many centuries. Freeman, slaves, monarchs, and dictators have all had their own definitions of freedom, most of them involving some description of the absence of restraint on human behavior. There may not be a good definition of freedom. Nevertheless, we need to have some definition to suit our purposes.

The Founding Fathers talked about natural rights:

"We hold these truths to be self-evident, that all men are created equal, that they are endowed by their Creator with certain unalienable Rights, that among these are Life, Liberty and the pursuit of Happiness."

This line, penned by Thomas Jefferson as the first sentence of the Declaration of Independence, is a statement of belief, not a declaration of an eternal truth. This statement is derived from millennia of debate on the subject of what freedom is and what it is not. It is by no means a perfect definition. Jefferson himself originally substituted the word *property* for the pursuit of happiness, and property rights - including rights over our own selves as property - are an essential part of freedom.

It is said that a free person has the right to engage in any behavior that does not infringe upon the rights of another. This is the basic philosophy behind Libertarianism, and it is a failure. No enduring government could be constructed under such a definition, for it borders both on anarchy and on democracy, neither of which have ever been successful in preserving individual freedom.

For example, do we have the right to operate a motor vehicle for our personal use if its operation pollutes the environment? If we buy something from someone else where we have information about that particular property that makes it valuable, do we have the right to take advantage of the seller's ignorance? Do we have the right to operate a motor vehicle at a very high rate of speed as long as we do not injure or harm other persons or property? There are thousands of such questions that cannot be answered by the simple libertarian argument, but which must be resolved through the creation and enforcement of appropriate laws.

No earthly system of government or law has ever been perfect in its ability to adequately and properly judge each circumstance and situation in which men find themselves. That doesn't mean we can't try to create such a system; it just means that all of our efforts will ultimately fall short. Perhaps that is why Jefferson made the statement that all men are created equal. Even though it is obvious that they are not *created* equal, under the system Jefferson was hoping to help establish all men would be *equal under the law*. It would be difficult to identify any other government in history founded upon that concept.

What about life, liberty, and the pursuit of happiness? We can draw many conclusions, some of them conflicting, from those three items. Jefferson's intent was not to define these terms but rather to state that he, and those who were the signers of the Declaration of Independence, believed these to be self-evident truths. That declaration made them rebels, for under the monarchy of King George they had no such rights. They were subject to the arbitrary whims of a distant monarch who was primarily interested in the New World as a source of revenue.

The right to life is just what it implies. All human beings in the United States have the right to life. There are no bounds put upon that right. Life is not defined as beginning at birth or conception or at any other moment, nor is it defined as ending once a person is no longer capable of fully caring for him or herself or at any other point of time. The point is that this declaration was radical, for it stated that men and women were free and should be protected by law from anything that would deprive them of life—even though life was not defined.

Liberty has more to do with freedom of movement, the freedom of gainful employment, the freedom of commerce and education and self-improvement. Liberty includes freedom of speech, freedom of the press, freedom of worship, and many of the other freedoms embodied in the Bill of Rights. Once again we arrive at the simplistic philosophy that says that we have these rights as long as we do not infringe upon others. Laws must be created to specify the boundary between personal rights so that one person may not infringe upon the rights of another.

The pursuit of happiness sounds like something we all understand, and yet it too is undefined in the declaration. It is a very lofty ideal and in some ways ties together the first two points and then expands them to create a general right of the freedom to pursue pretty much whatever one chooses. This was a radical idea, for throughout history most people have had little choice as to what they would do with their lives. Our Founding Fathers wanted Americans to have the opportunity to fulfill their potential and to find happiness as they defined it.

Jefferson was familiar with the writings of John Locke. Locke first published his *Second Treatise of Government* in 1690. In Chapter Two, "Of the state of nature," Locke describes the "state of nature" in which men exist before they create governments:

"The state of nature is ... a state of perfect freedom to order their actions and dispose of their possessions and persons as they see fit, within the bounds of the laws of nature, without asking leave or depending upon the will of any other man.

A state also of equality, wherein all the power and jurisdiction is reciprocal, no one having more than another; there being nothing more evident than that creatures of the same species and rank, promiscuously born to all the same advantages of nature and the use of the same faculties, should also be equal one amongst another without subordination or subjection ... .

The state of nature has a law of nature to govern it, which obliges every one; and reason, which is that law, teaches all mankind who will but consult it that, being all equal and independent, no one ought to harm another in his life, health, liberty, or possessions ... "

Like Jefferson, Locke was stating a belief about the law of nature, for no such laws existed unless they had been handed down by some supreme being. However, Locke went on to say that that law of nature is actually reason, which is nothing more than a philosophical concept.

What is important about all of this is that freedom must be defined in every generation. Freedom must be fought for and won, it must be maintained, and it must be protected. Natural laws may be just exactly that, but unless men act in accordance with them, they might as well not exist.

Therefore, Jefferson was making a statement of belief about a principle he held dear that flew in the face of established authority and government in his day, as it had in most prior days of human experience. Years later the Constitution was established with that same basis of inalienable rights and natural law in which Jefferson so fervently believed. If men and women are to participate in a free society it is vital that they voluntarily agree to observe the rules and laws of that society. If they do not, they not only violate the rights of those around them, but they destroy the law itself. We cannot be free when there is no profound respect for the rights of man and for the value and worth of the individual. Freedom does not demand that we sacrifice ourselves in the service of something supposedly greater than us. Freedom is not arbitrary, nor can it be removed in a moment.

We live in a country where freedom was once enshrined above all other things. Unfortunately freedom in America today looks a lot like that statue of Saddam Hussein US forces attempted to topple in Iraq; it has fallen, but it has yet to lose its grip on its foundation.

We lose a little freedom when government decides to impose a tax upon us. We lose more freedom when government decides to spend money to benefit a certain portion of the populace. We lose freedom when our government demands that our young men submit themselves to a draft and involuntary military service. We lose a little freedom when we create bureaucracies and agencies that dictate our actions if we should choose to get involved in things that come under their purview.

We lose freedom when our president writes an executive order and puts it into effect. We lose freedom when unjust judges impose obligations upon us that are not found in the Constitution or in the law. We lose freedom when our elected officials abandon the principle of integrity and their oath of office as they engage in bribery and corruption to gain power and influence over us.

We have the freedom to surrender our freedom, but we must then live with the consequences. If we made such a choice—and we have done so thousands of times over the past two centuries—at the very least all of those affected should have the opportunity to decide for themselves. However, our elected representatives often think they know better than we do or allow themselves to become coerced by their peers into actions that harm those they represent and damage the Constitution. It is the height of hypocrisy that so many of our elected officials feel free to vote themselves raises and benefits while they exempt themselves from the laws that they pass and impose upon us.

Today, the encroachments upon our freedom are legion. Each infringement is a theft that steals a little bit of our freedom. After two centuries of encroachments it is hard to realize how much we have lost. The PATRIOT Act is only one of the most egregious examples, and we failed to stand up to it because we were afraid. The PATRIOT Act took away our privacy and many of our rights so that in theory a small number of potential terrorists might be more easily identified.

When our government sees fit to engage in torture, *we become the enemy.* It is a very short step from imprisoning and torturing citizens of other countries because they are deemed to be potential terrorists to imprisoning and torturing American citizens. We feel frustrated that drug lords thrive and prosper, but if we illegally seize their property and offer no legal recourse, we have destroyed some of our own freedom. Governments seize and expand their power; they never voluntarily relinquish it.

Any weapon, legal or otherwise, can be used against us. Much as we may despise the Miranda ruling, which has freed so many thousands of criminal suspects, we should be encouraged by the development of new technologies and techniques that have made it possible to obtain solid convictions—when the police have the time and resources to use them, that is.

## The Freedom Spectrum

If we are educated about politics at all, we are told about the spectrum or continuum between conservatism and liberalism, or conservatism and socialism. We are told that these are the two extremes of political thought, but this is not correct. Here is what the political "spectrum" *really* looks like:

```
                        Constitutional
Anarchy     Democracy     Republic              Totalitarianism
   |_____|_____|_____|
```

Anarchy is the absence of government or the absence of law. No society can long exist in anarchy. At the other end, totalitarianism includes any form of state domination, such as monarchy, dictatorship, communism, socialism, and fascism.

Democracy, at least the way the ancient Greeks practiced it, is the closest form of organized government to anarchy. There is neither representative body nor executive, though there may be some form of judicial system in place. In terms of personal freedom, libertarianism as a political philosophy probably falls somewhere between democracy and constitutional republic.

If you understand this simple political spectrum, you already know more about the nature of government than many politicians. You understand that the function of government is to allow its citizens the maximum amount of freedom with a minimum of restraint. Free people are capable of exercising their own individual genius and can accomplish things that will improve all of society. The necessary freedoms include freedom of speech and press, freedom of worship, freedom of property, and sound, rigorously enforced contract law.

Over the past century, our federal government has moved our country a long way toward totalitarianism. What we have in America today is a welfare state that is more of a socialist government that a republican government. Our federal government believes that we as citizens and taxpayers are more like subjects than free and independent citizens. This belief is manifested to us every single day as we are burdened with more and more taxes, and our government makes decisions contrary to the will of the people.

Therefore, the question we must answer is how we can move our government back to the left of the political spectrum toward the constitutional republic the Founding Fathers created. First, the American people need to be educated about the great blessing that the Founding Fathers conferred upon us. Second, they need to be convinced that they would be better off under such a government. Third, they need to be motivated to become involved in the process that will lead us in the right direction. This may sound like compulsion, but that is not the intent, and it should not be the practice. It is more like helping an accident victim regain the ability to walk and then to run. Many men would choose freedom if offered the choice. Like the accident victim, our actions will be constrained until we learn to do once more those things of which we are at present incapable.

I believe that there are millions of Americans who will, when asked, join this struggle and commit time and resources to it. Our message to them is not about some way to cheat the government or take advantage of others, and it is not about a religion or a multilevel marketing campaign. Our message is about the natural rights of man, which have been taken from us piece by piece, so that the land of the free is today a mere shadow of its former self.

How will we bring this about? Each of us must make a personal commitment. We must make ourselves responsible for restoring our freedoms. We need to study the Constitution and the writings of the founders so that we understand their intent and their inspired work. With that knowledge we will be able to understand what our government is doing and know for ourselves whether its actions are Constitutional or not.

We need to commit our time and our resources to this important work. We need to take time away from our TVs and Blackberries and e-mail to read and ponder what it is that we have been given—and have almost discarded. We need to be people of integrity, wisdom, and compassion.

## What is Freedom?

History indicates that governments fall over time. Kingdoms rise and kingdoms fall; kingdoms grow and kingdoms shrink as war, famine, pestilence, and conquest bring about changes. Democracies usually self-destruct, often in less than two centuries. Tyranny is often overthrown and only rarely replaced with something that offers men greater freedom.

The Constitution of the United States could not have been established as the law of the land had there not been a revolution preceding its framing. Freedom had to be won, and free men need to keep on winning their freedom every single day. Threats to freedom come from within and without, for the power-hungry always want to enslave their brethren.

We understand that anarchy is the absence of government. No society can long endure in anarchy. It is like a vacuum that can only exist as long as it can successfully resist external pressures. We cannot call those living in anarchy free, for in such an environment they have no guarantees of personal liberty. By its own definition men are not governed by law in anarchy, which means that there is no protection of any natural rights.

We also understand that all forms of totalitarian government by definition repress personal freedom. It seems to be the case that all governments tend to become more repressive over time, with the rare exception of the "enlightened despot" who maintains a paternalistic attitude toward his subjects and takes certain steps to help them improve their situation. A totalitarian government may guarantee to its subjects certain rights, such as the right to employment, the right to housing, and the right to healthcare "guaranteed" to the people by Communist regimes. History clearly indicates that such regimes can never deliver on their promises, for they have taken away the incentive to produce and replaced it with dependency.

A popular philosophy in the 1920s was that a totalitarian government could provide cradle-to-grave support for its citizens. It can't, and neither can a free market society. As we will see in the next few pages, only a totalitarian society can hope to provide for its citizens' every need. One of the most important documents of the twentieth century, the Universal Declaration of Human Rights, specifically attempts to impose human rights on every nation throughout the world. Let's compare the two types of rights and see which one provides for greater freedom.

Our definition of freedom must be one that incorporates natural rights, those which in reality may not exist but which the Founding Fathers believed to exist. It must exclude "human rights," the type guaranteed in a welfare state. The reasoning is simple:

1. A free man or woman has the right to engage in those activities designed to promote life, liberty, and the pursuit of happiness, as long as those rights are not exercised at the expense of others.

2. There exist no rights that must be paid for by someone else.

Defining the first statement is extremely difficult; the definition varies with time, place, technology, and the organization of society. Defining the second is very simple, particularly if our federal government is confined to the rights specifically granted to it in the Constitution. Government should work for the common good and never for any minority or special interest group. The natural rights of those who belong to minorities must be protected as they are for the majority, but no class or group is to be granted any special privilege by virtue of their membership in that class or group.

These two statements conflict with the laws we have today, for much of that law violates either or both of the two statements. In other words, if Americans are to become free again, much of the laws currently on the books must be repealed. Likewise, every Federal court and Supreme Court decision must be carefully reviewed in light of the language of the Constitution, and appropriate adjustments or rescissions made. Both tasks are easier said than done, for in both cases the process, if it ever did take place, would be highly politicized. In fact, such a process could only take place when a high percentage of politically involved Americans have a thorough and comprehensive understanding of the Constitution.

# Human Rights versus Natural Rights

We need to understand that human rights are *not* an extension of natural rights. If anything, human rights as currently defined supplant and replace natural rights. The attempt to advance and enforce human rights is an attempt to replace God, for if every man were subject to the human rights found in the Universal Declaration suffering, greed, hunger, poverty, illiteracy, and self-determination would vanish from the earth—at least, until everything fell apart. Most people who claim to be religious believe that this life is a period of trial and testing where we prepare ourselves for a better life in the next phase of existence. Eliminating the negative aspects of mortal life may deprive life of its purpose and meaning.

To put it very simply:

*Natural* rights are the "I may work to improve my situation as I see fit" rights. If I don't work, I don't eat.

*Human* rights are "the world owes me a living" rights. I have the right to share in the fruit of your labors because I live on this planet. All the earth is the common property of its inhabitants.

In the next chapter we will explore this Declaration in more depth and try to understand the terrible effects it is having on the people of the world today.

Please note that we have not created a firm definition of what freedom is, nor should we expect to do so. Instead, we have placed ourselves in much the same position as the Founding Fathers when they were trying to determine what freedom was and how their definition could become part of the Constitution of the United States. We know what freedom isn't; it isn't the right to be cared for by the state. We're just not entirely sure of what freedom really *is*.

Now let's look at this Declaration, after which we will project current trends and see what this country will look like in the year 2015.

# CHAPTER THREE

# Citizens of the World

I t seems that whenever a nation goes through a period of trial and difficulty, when it emerges its people will re-examine their values. Difficult times can bring discouragement and disillusionment, as well as pain and fear. Often we want to try to ensure that we do not experience such things again. When the hard times come to an end, we may have lost the will to struggle, even when we need to rebuild our own lives.

This happened in the United States after the Civil War and, to a lesser extent, after World War I. During the Civil War, President Lincoln temporarily removed certain freedoms guaranteed in the Bill of Rights for certain individuals and groups and even imposed martial law on more than one occasion. All these things established precedents that would be revisited time and again in the years to come. Subsequent abuses of the Constitution would become more flagrant and affect many more people.

The latter part of the nineteenth century was characterized by massive industrialization, accompanied by the rape of the landscape and the growth of labor unions. No country had effectively dealt with the negative consequences of industrialization, with the rise of slums, the further stratification of society with the super-rich and the downtrodden workers, and the waste and destruction of natural resources and national treasures. The Framers certainly could not have envisioned the overwhelming changes that would come about nor their effect upon the American people and their way of life.

The first two decades of the twentieth century witnessed an unprecedented response to industrialization and its effect upon the masses. Unrest, poverty, and unhealthy working conditions prepared the working classes for socialism and communism, both of which were supposed to exalt the worker and amply reward him for his labors. Many in Europe and the United States debated these new philosophies, for we had not yet learned to fear them.

During the 1920s, Americans rejoiced at having ended The Great War and prided themselves on being great, noble, and free. For the moment, we rejected the notion of unifying the nations of the world in order to avoid further war and conflict, but we didn't do it for the right reasons. We should have rejected the League of Nations because it violated American sovereignty and because that organization did not support our concept of natural rights. Instead, the United States did not join the League of Nations primarily because the United States had decided not to ratify the Treaty of Versailles. Many Americans preferred the isolationist stance that George Washington had recommended and which had served us well.

Two decades later, as the world recovered from the Second World War, the people of the world wanted to see if there wasn't some way to make sure that wars would never again be fought. The United Nations was founded in 1945, and the United States Senate ratified the United Nations treaty in July of that year. Between the failure of the League of Nations and the founding of the United Nations, many people had changed the way they thought about politics, economics, and rights. Many were ready for a new, more Utopian way of life in which all men would be treated as equals and have the same opportunity to make of themselves whatever they wished. These were lofty thoughts and high ideals, but their foundation was sinister and very dangerous.

Men and women now created a new "generation" of rights. The first generation consisted of the natural rights, which were associated with the Enlightenment and particularly the American Revolution. Natural rights, as we have mentioned previously, include the rights to life and liberty and the rights to freedom of speech and worship, among others.

The second generation of rights, which expanded into the social, cultural, and economic areas, was associated with the problems of unregulated capitalism, and they include the right to work and the right to an education. Now, with the Universal Declaration of Human Rights issued by the United Nations in 1948, the third generation of rights has been enthroned. This group of "rights" includes the collective rights to political self-determination and economic development.

The United States Congress initially paid little attention to the Declaration. It was not a treaty, and as a declaration it did not require ratification. However, in the sixty years since its creation, more and more governments around the world have adopted large chunks of the Declaration into their constitutions and/or utilized the Declaration as guidance in amending their existing legislation.

It didn't take long for Congress to realize that they could greatly expand the power of the federal government by taking advantage of the favorable feelings many Americans had toward the Declaration. They began to use the Declaration as if it superseded and encompassed the Constitution, which it clearly did not.

Here are a couple of examples of human rights as found in the Universal Declaration of Human Rights:

Article 22

Everyone, as a member of society, has the right to social security and is entitled to realization, through national effort and international co-operation and in accordance with the organization and resources of each State, of the economic, social and cultural rights indispensable for his dignity and the free development of his personality.

Even though there is a difference between "social security" as described above and Social Security as we understand it, there can be little doubt that this article flies in the face of our natural rights as described in the Constitution and in the writings of the Founding Fathers.

### Article 23

Everyone who works has the right to just and favourable remuneration ensuring for himself and his family an existence worthy of human dignity, and supplemented, if necessary, by other means of social protection.

This is another very popular socialist notion, devoid of specific definitions and leaving the door open to individuals making impossible demands upon their government for their maintenance and support.

### Article 25

Everyone has the right to a standard of living adequate for the health and well-being of himself and of his family, including food, clothing, housing and medical care and necessary social services, and the right to security in the event of unemployment, sickness, disability, widowhood, old age or other lack of livelihood in circumstances beyond his control.

This is a classic definition of a welfare state. The underlying assumption is that all governments suppress their people and treat them as subjects while denying them opportunities for self-improvement. Placing the United Nations' stamp of approval on the document gave tremendous weight to its pronouncements, regardless of how ill-conceived and destructive they were. By the time the Declaration was signed, these ideas had been featured prominently throughout the United States for decades, and Americans were ready to receive them with open arms.

Human rights were proclaimed as a higher law, and the world assumed that government had the responsibility to be our brother's keeper. For some reason—and it is easy to imagine why—the downside was never disclosed. No one ever mentioned what would happen when people realized they didn't have to work, and that if they did their efforts were not rewarded. It was a much easier sell to tell people they would be cared for cradle to grave, instead of saying that the middle class would be taxed out of existence and most of the nation would descend into chaos and poverty.

What other doctrine could be so powerful and so persuasive as to move Americans away from their Constitution, their religious faith, their morals, and their integrity? If you don't carefully think through each of the principles in the Declaration, you can come away with the mistaken belief that these are worthy, attainable principles. The world was turned upside down at that time anyway; after the greatest conflict in human history, the United States made friends and generously rebuilt our former enemies, while we renewed our animosity and hatred toward our former ally, the Soviet Union. It was a time when traditional values were under fire, for we were taught that they had failed to prevent the terrible conflict that had just ended.

Perhaps you had an experience similar to mine when you were growing up. I was in public schools in the 1950s and 1960s. I cannot recall being taught about the Constitution, but I do remember being taught about the wonderful United Nations, and how the world was going to be united. It was years later when I realized the significance of those teachings, and it is only now as I write this that I grasp their full impact.

Of course, back in those days we still waved the flag and honored our veterans. We still talked about duty to God and to country. I learned to revere those who had paid the ultimate price so that I might live in freedom. But then the United States seemed to lose its way. Korea was a turning point, an undeclared war with terrible losses on both sides, which has yet to be brought to a successful conclusion half a century later. We blundered into Vietnam, fighting a war on behalf of the French when they found the situation untenable. We remain the only nation ever to use nuclear weapons on an enemy, and on primarily civilian populations at that. We were told we should feel guilty about having done so regardless of the American lives those weapons probably saved.

The call for human rights found many listening ears. Who didn't want to abolish poverty, ignorance, sickness, hunger, and fear? Who could stand up against the notion that all men deserve to have everything given to them? Who would be foolish enough to argue with those who wanted to give men all that they had sought for throughout human history?

There was only one problem with all this. In order to get men to freely give all that was needed to support these "rights," coercion and force were required. Giving human rights to one person must mean taking them from someone else. It means denying natural rights to all. Ultimately, any government enforcing human rights must enslave all its citizens and self-destruct in a vain attempt to give everything to those who will not work.

Let's compare the effects on a nation governed by natural rights and one governed by more expansive human rights. Following is a rather imperfect progression of events in two different worlds. In both cases all things are equal except for their government. However, in the first instance natural rights are enshrined; in the other, human rights.

# Natural Rights

A strong work ethic is one of the founding
principles of society, and is advocated by
government and all public institutions.

↓

Property rights are fully respected.

↓

The central government is relatively small and weak, and
fulfills only those functions necessary to the preservation of
the natural rights of its citizens, including defending its citizens both from external aggression and internal subversion.

↓

There are multiple social classes covering the
entire economic spectrum. The boundaries
between classes are arbitrary and fluid.

↓

Taxes are minimal, and are assessed only as needed
to support the essential functions of government.

↓

Governments at all levels encourage and incentivize philan-
thropy and charitable work to help lift the poor and the needy.

↓

Poverty is diminished by abundant economic
opportunity, and because all who can labor must do so
in order to support themselves and their families.

↓

Economic opportunity increases wealth, and all classes benefit.

↓

The creation of wealth by a few encourages many to
follow their example and create wealth for themselves.

↓

The country thrives. Because the government has created
and maintained an environment in which any may
prosper, dissension and strife are significantly reduced.

↓

The country makes significant economic and technological progress, and its citizens are encouraged to improve themselves and voluntarily serve others.

# Human Rights

In order for any government to grant unto its citizens the full spectrum of human rights, the government must ensure that no one will fall through the huge social safety net that must be created.

↓

The government provides cradle-to-grave support for all of its citizens.

↓

Property rights may exist initially, and laws regarding property may remain on the books indefinitely, but the government must have a claim on enough of its citizens' assets in order to guarantee human rights to all.

↓

The central government is strong and large, for it must look into and micro-manage every aspect of life to ensure that there is no suffering, poverty, or want.

↓

The people are divided into two classes; the governing elite and all the rest. Those who are wealthy will have fled the country as soon as they realized that their government could seize everything from them.

↓

The government heavily taxes its citizens and redistributes the proceeds after funneling them through massive bureaucracies.

↓

Citizens begin to realize that they are not going to be allowed to keep the fruits of their labors, and they either leave the country for greener pastures or abandon their work ethic and allow themselves to be cared for.

↓

With the decline in the number of wealthy in the country, taxes must be increased on all the remainder who are still paying taxes.

↓

As the incentive to work diminishes, citizens begin
to grab all they can from government. Government
bureaucracies must increase in size in order to
handle increased numbers of beneficiaries.

↓

Poverty increases as more and more citizens take
advantage of the free ride government is offering.

↓

A crisis develops as tax receipts decline and benefits payouts
increase. Government debt grows and becomes permanent.

↓

The quality of education declines for all citizens.
The quality of health care declines for all citizens.
The quality of government services declines for all citizens.

↓

A downward spiral accelerates as cracks
appear in this Utopian veneer:

- The quality of life plummets as illiteracy rises and
  the citizens become completely self-indulgent.

- The economy grinds to a halt, for the means of production
  and distribution have both been taken over by government.

- Rationing is everywhere, which brings
  about unrest and dissent.

- Crime increases as frustrated people look
  for any outlet to vent their anger.

- The nation itself may start a war with some hapless country
  just to shift attention away from the ineptitude of its leaders.

↓

Eventually the country goes bankrupt and self-destructs,
all in the name of social progress and human rights.

# A Recipe for Disaster

It is hard to imagine a better or faster way to destroy a nation, a race, or even a species than by implementing the subversive and dangerous doctrines found in this Universal Declaration of Human Rights. All that mankind has accomplished will be wiped out as we apply these seemingly high-minded ideals, and they take us back to the law of the jungle. When the state has been tasked with maintaining the health and well-being of all of its citizens, those citizens have become subjects, and they will soon become slaves.

Based upon this brief discussion, can there be any doubt that "human rights" is simply another name for slavery? If everyone is provided for by government, government becomes the source of all the people have. In order to provide all the people have, the government must steal or extort it from others. This creates an endless demand upon those who continue to work or produce. Ultimately the state must own everything including the means of production, for the demands made by the people will always be greater than it can meet.

Human rights mean the end of law, for it removes the foundation of order every society must possess. Human rights by definition must transcend national boundaries so that all may share equally. It means the end of nations and the creation of a super government that will rule with an iron fist in redistributing—and squandering—the world's dwindling wealth.

## Americans Are Becoming Citizens of the World

The other primary purpose of the United Nations is to unify the nations of the earth—in a political sense if possible, in an economic sense in any event. For millennia people have migrated from one place to another in search of a better life. Millions have come to America for just that reason, and for the most part they have been made welcome. America has been more than generous to tens of millions of immigrants, and the greatest gift we have given them is the opportunity to make something of themselves, free from the restrictions and bonds that held them down in their former countries.

If the Universal Declaration of Human Rights were to become the law of the land—and clearly all three branches of our federal government act as if it already were—millions more would want to come here. This time, however, they would not be coming to create a better life; they would be coming to be taken care of.

The world would be divided into the "haves" and the "have-nots," and those in the "have-not" nations would do everything they could to get to one of the "have" nations. There would have to be a substantial body of international law to deal with these issues, and in all likelihood those laws would mandate that the "have" nations would share their abundance with the "have-nots." This could be viewed as something of a bribe, with the implicit promise that all those huddled masses would not appear at our doors as long as we pay them off to stay in their own countries. Longer-term, it seems obvious that the trend for the elimination of national and state boundaries would accelerate. After all, if all men fall under the Universal Declaration, what need do we have with national governments when a single world government would be so much more efficient?

Besides, we would need new bureaucracies to ensure that the distribution of natural resources and wealth was balanced and fair. These bureaucracies would have to have powers that span the entire planet, for all men have been granted equal human rights.

Let's leave this fantasy world, which is rapidly approaching, and sum up. The Universal Declaration of Human Rights poses three major threats to the entire human race:

1.  The Declaration gives governments a license to steal, for they point to the "higher law," which mandates that all men are equal and must be treated as if they were equal. In order to treat them equally government must eliminate property rights, for all that its citizens own must be available for redistribution to others.

2. The Declaration can only be fully implemented when nations cease to exist so that all men may be truly equal.

3. The Declaration has tremendous appeal to the vast majority of the human race. Some of us think we are entitled to share in what others make. Some of us want to get even for having been born in the Third World. Some people actually believe that we can create a Utopia on earth. Many simply don't care about the philosophy; they just want all those benefits without having to earn them.

There may even be a fourth threat, and it might be the biggest threat of all. It is so easy to negatively label anyone foolish enough to speak out against human rights. We used to say that Social Security was the "third rail" of politics; speak against it, and your political career dies instantly. If we are to save our Constitution, our country, our freedom, our planet, and ourselves, we must find a way to effectively speak out against human rights. Talk about having no constituency.

## CHAPTER FOUR

# America in 2015

S cience fiction writers generally write about something that will happen fifteen to twenty years in the future, and they often take advantage of new and upcoming technologies of which few people are aware. They often get involved in "trend extrapolation," which sounds pretty complex but is actually quite simple. When you extrapolate a trend, you merely continue it for an indefinite period of time. Unfortunately, real life doesn't work that way; trends change, and trends come and go.

I find that many Americans are unaware of the ways in which their freedom is restricted. Many others are unaware of the myriad laws and regulations we are compelled to obey, ignorance of which is no excuse. In this chapter I will extrapolate some current trends and incorporate the two ideas I just mentioned to give you a picture of what life will probably be like in these United States just a few short years from now. I will focus on the following areas:

- The Economy
- The Deficit
- The National Debt now

- Taxes
- Social Security and Medicare
- Government control of business
- The Federal Reserve
- The Dollar
- Personal freedom
- Property seizures
- Health care
- Public education
- The War on Terror

It will not be a pretty picture. I hope this chapter will cause you to ask yourself this question:

What will I tell my children and grandchildren when they ask what it *used* to be like to be free?

# A look into America's Future—a "Report" from 1 July 2015

In 2013 inflation returned with a vengeance. The United States moved from a deflationary depression—which worsened dramatically between 2010 and 2012—into a period of Jimmy Carter-style "stagflation." With economic activity still in the doldrums, our national savings rate still close to zero, and the tremendous losses upon losses experienced by millions of Americans in their retirement accounts as stock markets continued to deteriorate, rapidly rising prices were about the last thing Americans needed.

Ordinarily, prices don't rise very much during a depression, for demand is significantly reduced. Economics 101 dictates that price is a function of supply and demand, and if *demand* falls and *supply* remains the same, *price* must fall. That's not happening now. Price inflation has returned for two reasons: There are too many dollars chasing too few goods, and world supplies of a wide range of raw materials are rapidly dwindling. Much of what is still available has been siphoned off by the world's new superpower, China.

Unemployment remains at about 20 percent; at least, that's the number the federal government acknowledges. The real number is probably much higher. Just as it did during the Great Depression in the 1930s, the federal government spent vast sums of money to try to deal with unemployment, but every program failed to create any meaningful number of jobs. Because the programs were so terribly expensive, our deficits soared to new and astronomic heights.

Each year's deficit was added to the mushrooming national debt, which by now has no hope of being repaid even three generations from now. It is clear that at some point in time the dollar will collapse, and there is a great fear that the rate of inflation will rise to the point where we actually experience hyperinflation. Because that had happened on two previous occasions in American history, it was never out of the question; however, no living American has any memory of the last time our currency experienced hyperinflation.

American troops remain in more than one hundred countries around the world, but their presence is seldom viewed as beneficial. Instead, American military presence in a country looks more like a veiled threat from a country that seems increasingly desperate to shift blame for its failure to solve its own problems.

With the collapse of the Cantarell oilfield in Mexico, millions more Mexicans made their way into the United States. However, these millions were not able to assimilate quickly into American society as their predecessors had done; these newcomers found America torn by political divisions and damaged by an ongoing economic crisis. They also found a changing mood among the American people and a growing anger toward these immigrants who, despite being encouraged and rewarded by the Democratic Party, were now viewed with suspicion and distrust. Their presence put an ever-greater strain on the social safety net, which only remains in place because the Federal Reserve is printing so many dollars to give to them.

The real-estate markets remain in the doldrums, for demand is low. Household formation has declined as fewer people are getting divorces, fewer people are getting married, fewer people are raising children, and more and more households are having three and even four generations under one roof. The government has tried repeatedly to prop up failing lenders and failing builders, but it is unlikely that either will become profitable in the foreseeable future. These companies were deemed "too big to fail"; there was widespread acknowledgment that if they failed, the American people would have no opportunity to pull themselves out of this greater depression.

The free enterprise system is in tatters throughout the United States. From the moment that the federal government "rescued" General Motors, the heavy hand of government acted very much like Soviet central planning. It not only did permanent damage to the former General Motors, but it damaged the entire automobile industry. Ford found it almost impossible to compete with a company that had the deep pockets of government sponsorship. Foreign car companies were put under tremendous pressure by the government as the regulators played the "Buy American" card. This in turn put a strain on our relations with countries with whom we had previously been friendly, including Japan and South Korea.

The other "unintended consequence" of the government's takeover of General Motors has been to significantly reduce the appeal of America as a place for foreigners to invest. Sovereign wealth funds for many countries had been sending money to the United States to purchase shuttered factories and other equipment which could put tens of thousands of Americans back to work. In America the new anti-business environment with its myriad regulations and high taxes, coupled with the federal government's powerful support of labor unions, stopped that flow of funds completely and diverted it to more business-friendly shores.

One of the things that continue to depress real estate prices are property taxes. Despite the ongoing consolidation of local and county governments all over the country to stave off impending bankruptcies, taxing authorities have had no choice but to dramatically raise property taxes and every other form of taxes they could. Most highways have become toll roads, though with so many people unemployed and so few having the funds for leisure travel with gasoline at $9.00 a gallon, the highways are relatively empty.

America was forced to adapt the European style system of taxing energy, with the result that gasoline taxes doubled and tripled in a very short period of time. Of course, it didn't help when crude oil went to $250 a barrel and then fell off a few dollars before rising even further. Today no one has any idea how high the price of oil will rise, but with 700 million Indians and almost a billion Chinese hitting the roads for the very first time the price of crude oil can only go up.

Besides, governments at all levels are perpetually strapped for cash. The federal government continues to spend as if there were no tomorrow, and at this point it seems they may be right. State governments are required by their own constitutions to balance their budgets, but without huge bailouts from the federal government most states would be bankrupt at this point.

Leaders of the federal government seem relatively unconcerned with the debt burdens of the states, partially because the federal government has set up a regional system of government that could, and appears to be, overruling and reducing the authority of the states.

The average American is making less in real dollars than at any time in the past one hundred years, and for the privilege he is working for the government for the first nine months of each year. Taxes have risen so high that it takes nine months of a person's income just to pay all of his taxes.

Because of the ongoing depression and now the high rate of consumer price inflation, Americans are far from prosperous. They are unhappy and discontented, and they are fearful about the future. For many the only choice is to give up and become a ward of the state, allowing the government to dictate every aspect of their lives. This is the "mess of pottage" choice, and all it does is keep starvation at bay.

Tens of millions of Americans had virtually all of their life savings tied up in their retirement accounts, and after the market fell dramatically and they lost well over half their value—and with it any hope they may have had of enjoying their retirement—the federal government stepped in and nationalized the remainder of their retirement funds. This left most Americans completely without savings and almost completely dependent upon the government. Millions of Americans today are walking a tightrope; if their income is diminished by as little as 10 percent they will not survive. The American middle class has all but disappeared.

You have to ask yourself how the federal government can survive when it runs ever-growing deficits year after year, shows not the slightest sense of fiscal responsibility, and abdicates many of its responsibilities or turns them over to parties who have no constitutional authority to hold them. Why haven't the American people risen up and exercised their sovereign authority, restoring America to its constitution and removing those who are to blame from their positions of power?

The answers are very simple. First, at no point in time were enough Americans in any part of the country sufficiently united that they could effect positive change. Second, the American people responded to crisis after crisis by "hunkering down" and hoping that things would get better. They didn't. Third, Americans have been led to believe that their government is there to help them. That's what the "social safety net" is all about. Our federal government has promised to "be there for us" no matter what happens, and has clearly given the impression that it can do just about anything. Of course, we forget the effects of hurricane Katrina and the complete failure of government to be able to get people back on their feet. Americans became fearful to the point that many felt that standing up and asking important questions of our leaders might not just "rock the boat," it might bring retaliation.

What the American people didn't know, or at least didn't fully comprehend, was that a long series of American presidents had converted the United States from a Constitutional Republic to a powerful national government that reached into every aspect of our lives. One by one our freedoms were taken away and replaced with government guarantees. We didn't realize that this is how governments become powerful—by buying the votes and the loyalty of those it was supposed to serve. Our national government allowed educational standards to slip and created generation after generation of increasingly illiterate and uneducated citizens. People without a proper education in the art of government are unqualified to be responsible citizens. They are only capable of being enslaved.

The government concealed its profligacy, ineptitude, foolishness, and dishonesty by quickly changing America from the wealthiest nation in the world to the biggest debtor in the history of the world. The process took less than two generations, because once it was commenced, the "have-nots" got organized and got their elected representatives to strip America of the wealth it had taken two centuries to accumulate. America itself became enslaved by its own burden of debt, which brought about the loss of its sovereignty. *Sovereignty* was never considered to be a very important word by the American people until it was lost.

The government functioned smoothly as it suppressed dissent and created one crisis after another to keep Americans off balance. America was like one massive earthquake with frequent, irregular aftershocks. What had once passed for normal in American life was replaced by numerous ongoing emergencies. Morality, decency, integrity, and fairness were all swept aside as government revealed its true face. The face of government became the facelessness of the welfare state, identified only by those who grabbed the headlines and gave "photo ops" when they wanted to lecture the American people. Government became a cartel, a monopoly, having no competition and becoming ever more powerful and intrusive.

Finally, a candidate for the office of president of the United States announced his plan to wreak havoc on the American consciousness by invoking "shock and awe" against the American people[1]. Most Americans cheered, for this would be a powerful stroke that would open the floodgates of government largesse. It would shower wealth beyond measure upon the American people.

"Shock and awe" is a military term, one utilized by the United States in the conduct of its war against Saddam Hussein in Iraq. "Shock and awe" means destroying the enemy's ability to resist, and it involves far more than bombing command and control centers. It means creating a crisis in which government, citizens, and the military become powerless to resist because they see nothing but chaos and confusion all around them.

In a psychological sense, "shock and awe" refers to destroying a person's or a society's collective memory of life as it once was. If you wish to replace a legitimate form of government through a coup, the best way to do it is to cause the people to forget how their government was meant to operate. Lenin did this in Russia by taking advantage of tremendous unrest in that country, made worse by the seeming neglect and lack of compassion on the part of the tsar. Once Russia was fully and disastrously engaged in World War I, Lenin had his opportunity to take advantage of the confusion, unrest, terrible economic conditions, and the real possibility of Russia being defeated by Germany to wrest power from the tsar and institute a new and illegal government.

The same thing happened in the United States, though over a much longer period of time. Under the control of the National Education Association (NEA), the national teacher's union, American public schools began filling the heads of their students with everything but academics. Citizenship, history, literacy, humanities, and science were downplayed and degraded, while sex education, sensitivity, situation ethics, witchcraft, and self-esteem took their place. It was no surprise when Finland took first or second place in international academic competitions in the mid-2000s, while America ranked dead last in academics but first in self-esteem. Surely, no people ever felt prouder of their ignorance.

This was a major step in converting America from a constitutional republic to a socialist welfare state. Each successive president and Congress put another nail or two into the coffin of the Constitution by convincing Americans that we could easily afford to rob the rich to help the poor. Just as a law had to be passed in Great Britain to prevent medical doctors from leaving the British Isles, so laws had to be passed in America to prevent the wealthy from renouncing their citizenship and taking their wealth to some friendlier shore.

You see, in America, taxation follows citizenship. Whether you reside in the United States or not, and regardless of where you make your living, if you are an American citizen you are liable for income taxes on all of your earnings. To prevent the mass exodus of the wealthy, back in the 1990s Congress passed a law levying an immediate tax of 50 percent of the entire net worth of Americans who renounced their citizenship to move elsewhere.

The people applauded, for didn't the wealthy have an obligation to share what they had earned through their diligence? Why should they be allowed to take their ill-gotten gains somewhere else and not pay taxes? After all, capitalism is inherently evil, isn't it? And didn't the wealthy make all that money by exploiting others?

It was through insidious notions like these, repeated endlessly by ideologues, liberals, socialists, and Communists, that the American people began to change their basic beliefs. Why work hard to provide for yourself and your family when the government was always there to tax you? The government was never a partner in your enterprise, but it took a large chunk of your profits. If you didn't make any money the government never gave you anything back to help keep you going. In some jurisdictions the government taxed your *revenues*, which meant that you paid taxes whether you made a profit or not.

Besides, the government rewarded those who didn't work. The welfare laws were set up to destroy families and to free fathers from their obligation to their children. If the government didn't believe we should take responsibility for ourselves, why should we? Why not take the government for every penny you could? After all, it's the government's money, and dozens of books are being published about how you can get your share. Many agencies of the government actively solicit new recipients so that they may increase their budget, their staff, and their power.

As the spark of individual initiative hovered at the point of extinction, Americans were impacted by two very different forces. The one was government, which promised to take care of us as long as we gave up more of our freedom. The other was the declining pull of morality, which caused millions to enter destructive lifestyles and create dysfunctional families. The bedrock of society was being torn apart.

The self-proclaimed "elite" had formed generations ago in America as our abundance of natural resources combined with the Industrial Revolution to create immense wealth for a privileged few. As is almost always the case when people become wealthy, they lose sight of what is really important and often seek out ideas that are preposterous or even criminally misguided. Wealthy Americans threw money at eugenics, Communism, socialism, myriad experiments in social engineering and restructuring, and much more in their attempt to create a society unlike any the world had ever seen.

The subversion of our constitutional government came about quite simply through a series of crises. The elites wanted power, control, and immense wealth. They bought influence directly or through their corporations and trusts, and they saw to it that Americans were repeatedly told how much better off they would be in this "brave new world" they were creating. High-sounding ideas like the elimination of poverty, the eradication of disease, free public education, "a chicken in every pot and a car in every garage" appealed to Americans as they tried to rebound from world wars, financial panics, the Great Depression, currency crises, inflation, and much more.

In the midst of each crisis there was someone there to give them a helping hand, to make it easier for them to get back on their feet. What we failed to notice as we grew ever more dependent on this helping hand was that each bit of assistance was accompanied by higher taxes, more regulation, a bigger national debt, declining educational standards, and less individual freedom. The individual had to sacrifice some of his or her individuality in order to fit into this New World Order. Not to worry, though; once we got used to the new regime we wouldn't miss a little freedom.

There is much more to this picture, but by now you are beginning to understand. What you need to know is that *much of what has been discussed in the previous paragraphs has already come to pass.*

## If you really wanted to destroy freedom in America...

While we are on the subject of "thought experiments," let's talk about how you would go about destroying a free country like the United States under its Constitution. I'm not going to talk about conspiracies. Neither am I going to talk about how the nature of American life has changed as the self-styled elites have sprung up and impose their often ridiculous ideas upon this country. I just want to point out some of the steps it would be appropriate to take if someone really wanted to destroy our Constitutional government and even our country.

If you wanted to destroy freedom in America and move the United States from the first world to the third world, how would you go about it?

It would take many years of work to accomplish such a thing, requiring more than one generation. It would be a very long time before any person could say that the work of destruction was complete, in part because so many steps would need to be taken. Here are some of the things such a person or group might have on their to-do list:

## *The economy*

1. Create an independent bank and give it power over the currency. This gives the government enormous power over the people as it robs them of any financial security they may hope to have.

2. Debase the currency and remove any precious metals backing, thus giving this independent national bank the means to destroy the currency.

3. Support the currency through jawboning, arm-twisting, and bullying. Make it look like the currency still has value even when it is being deliberately and systematically destroyed by the government. This enables the government to retain power longer before the people rise up and exercise their rights as proclaimed in the Declaration of Independence.

4. Destroy the nation's industrial base. Hamstring it with innumerable regulations and saddle it with terribly burdensome costs and taxes so that industries are literally forced to move overseas.

5. Engage in a program of wealth redistribution. Begin the program with emotional appeals for compassion upon those who are less fortunate.

6. Convert the wealth of the nation into debt. Make the American people dependent upon their government. Regulate every aspect of their lives, take away all their privacy, suppress the worth of the individual in favor of the "greater good," and suspend basic constitutional freedoms whenever you want to.

## National politics

1. Chip away at the Constitution by enacting, writing, and creating one unconstitutional piece of legislation, Executive Order, or court ruling after another to cause confusion among the people and shift political power to the national government.

2. Destroy the system of checks and balances carefully built into the Constitution by the Founding Fathers. Have each branch of government overstep its Constitutional bounds, usurp authority, and ignore its responsibility to hold in check itself and both other branches.

3. Destroy the authority of the states by illegally initiating an unconstitutional system of regional governments. Fund the regional operations with federal funds and gradually put county and state governments out of business by transferring their authority.

4. Form an alliance between politicians and unions so that elected officials are always in the pocket of the union leaders. Unions tend to be predatory in their demands, and their leadership tends to be corrupt. Ensure that union membership is mandatory in as many fields of employment as possible, so that union leaders will exert enormous influence in the halls of power.

5. Bend the rules of government and justify doing so in order to overrule those pesky voters and get things done that "the people" want done.

# Social policy

1. Provide ever-larger and ever-expanding "social safety net" programs funded with tax dollars. When people know they can be fully cared for by the government, they will never again have any incentive to work or to provide for themselves and their families. Therefore, welfare "needs" will only grow.

2. Take away the right of the people to defend themselves from criminals and from their government.

3. In the name of "tolerance" ensure that no racial, ethnic, or religious groups are allowed to have any power over others. This will serve to remove all religious and moral influences from government. Quietly favor those groups that can deliver votes.

4. Encourage greed and consumerism. Repeal laws that would restrict behaviors once considered to be immoral or improper. Give the people the opportunity to make whatever choices they wish, with no obligation to be decent, moral, upright, or to be responsible citizens.

5. Create new and contradictory rules of behavior that favor one particular group over another. This will cause great confusion among the people, and they will become ever more disrespectful and un-trusting of government.

6. Create gross inequities in the public realm. Throw enormous amounts of money at giant corporations by labeling them "too big to fail," then throw even more money at those who refuse to care for themselves. This will ultimately condition Americans to see themselves as serfs, subjects to an all-powerful government which controls every aspect of their lives.

7. When the "social safety net" is about to bankrupt the country, raise taxes and steal the remaining wealth of the American middle class to postpone the day of reckoning.

## Resource crises

1. Deplete and squander the nation's natural resources until America is completely dependent upon other countries for everything it consumes.

2. Instead of establishing national policies of conservation and the intelligence use of resources, encourage waste. Encourage Americans to develop spending habits that become unsustainable. Refuse to allow Americans to exploit the vast untapped resources still available domestically under the pretense of "protecting the environment" or "keeping the wilderness pristine."

## Diplomacy

1. Wield a big stick as a nation, and become a bully in world affairs. Throw the nation's weight around and act not only as if we were the world's policeman, but as if we were the world's moral example.

2. Chip away at American sovereignty by replacing American law with international law or United Nations laws and regulations. Undermine the authority of our courts and our Congress by finding ways to subject Americans to new rules and laws imposed from outside the United States.

## Education

1. Degrade the public education system throughout the country so that integrity, morality, civic duty, and personal responsibility are dropped from the curriculum, along with the study of government and the Constitution. Replace them with classes on sex education, controlled substances, situation ethics, and self-esteem. The only behaviors that should be studied in public schools are deviant behaviors; the only government that should

be studied is socialism; the only religions that should be promoted are witchcraft, devil worship, and Islam.

2. Teach our children that the Founding Fathers were thieves, murderers, hypocrites, and oppressive slaveowners, and that they were interested solely in accumulating wealth and power for themselves.

3. Portray those in public life who are politically correct as being saints (despite their obvious flaws). Portray those who believe in traditional values as "backward," "Luddites," "reactionaries," "evil," "subversive," "uncaring," and "lacking human warmth or compassion."

4. Downplay the importance of academic excellence in favor of self-esteem, safe sex, newly-invented "rights," and proper use of illegal drugs. Teach them that the government owes them a living, that if they fail the government is always there to help them, and that they are free to do whatever they want with their lives even if their behavior benefits no one including themselves.

## *The media*

1. Employ the major media as a propaganda arm of government, using them to promote the ideas of socialism disguised as compassion, and making those in power who are corrupt and venal appear as Saints for all the wonderful things they have done for the American people.

2. Create an atmosphere of fear in the country. Make sure that the media and the politicians are constantly warning us of one danger or another. That will keep us off balance and make it more difficult for the people to unite around a common cause and require government to do what it was hired to do.

## Shock and awe

1. Refuse to address the ever-growing problems the nation faces, many of which have been created by the government. Delay action to resolve them as long as possible. When the problems become so critical that they must be addressed, an opportunity to seize more power has been created.

2. Take advantage of crises like natural disasters to convey the message that Americans must set aside their individuality in favor of the common good, and that government is the only solution to resolving crises.

3. Create economic, political and military crises wherever possible to create the impression that the people are too ignorant to understand the world in which they live, and consequently are helpless. This means that they must surrender more and more power to the government which is only interested in taking care of them. It also divides them, for government is involved in so many areas beyond its authority no two people can agree on the magnitude of the problem, much less a useful approach to fixing them.

4. Suppress the growing dissent among the taxpayers. Threaten their livelihoods, their lives, and their families. Strip them of all privacy, force them to pay for things contrary to their closest-held beliefs, terrorize them by illegally seizing their property, make an example of a few by depriving them of all their Constitutional rights, label them as "terrorists," "hate-mongers," "ignorant," "unpatriotic," and "Astroturf," and recruit the media to humiliate them.

5. Ensure that political leaders and the media constantly change the subject, ignore the issues, and employ name-calling[2] in order to pressure Americans to give up on their cherished beliefs and surrender to an overwhelming tide of greed, corruption, lies, duplicity, and manipulation.

6. Create an enormous web of regulations such that no American can understand or obey them all. Make them contradictory and arbitrarily enforceable. Replace the courts with unconstitutional bureaucratic tribunals invested with tremendous power. Use these regulations to deprive Americans of their rights and freedom.

7. Take away the self-sufficiency of those who are hard workers and who believe in what America can be. Make it increasingly difficult for Americans to take care of themselves. Tax their labors more and more so that they can never accumulate wealth.

8. Make Americans feel powerless to control their own destiny. Encourage the idea that life really has no purpose except to enjoy ourselves and get all that we can while the getting is good.

There are ways to short-circuit and hasten the process. "Shock and awe" is one of them, and it may have its effect in eliminating the influence of the last generation who have a significant knowledge of American history and the Constitution.

All of these things are in progress today. These influences and forces have been, for the most part, deliberately introduced into this country by those who would do us harm. Until now, Americans have not been able to successfully fend them off. We can do so, we must do so, and we must begin immediately. Our children and their children are all depending upon us.

# ★★★ Part Two ★★★

## America Today

"The assumption that spending more of the taxpayers' money will make things better has survived all kinds of evidence that it has made things worse. The black family—which survived slavery, discrimination, poverty, wars and depressions—began to come apart as the federal government moved in with its well-financed programs to 'help.'"

"The welfare state is not really about the welfare of the masses. It is about the egos of the elites."

—Thomas Sowell

## CHAPTER FIVE

# Our Welfare State

The United States in 2010 is much more of a welfare state than it is a Constitutional republic. We need to understand what a welfare state is and how it suppresses freedom, including property and other natural rights.

> "A democracy cannot exist as a permanent form of government ... [Eventually], the majority always votes for the candidates promising the most benefits from the public Treasury, with the result that a democracy always collapses over loose fiscal policy ... The world's greatest civilizations have progressed through this sequence: from bondage to spiritual faith; from spiritual faith to great courage; from great courage to liberty; from liberty to abundance; from abundance to selfishness; from selfishness to complacency; from complacency to apathy; from apathy to dependence; from dependency back again to bondage."
>
> —*Andrew Tyler Fraser*

America today is well into the "apathy to dependence" phase and working hard to enter the "dependency back again into bondage" phase. This is a natural progression, but it can be accelerated by those who seek to bring people into bondage, because they will gain power and wealth as a result. We must not underestimate the appeal of power. It may not have great hold upon you or me, but it affects many millions of people.

We need only look at dictatorships and totalitarian societies throughout history to discover that certain people seek power, people in power seek more power, and most of those in power are corrupted by it so that they bend the will of the people to meet their own desires.

Such people will literally rape their countries in their lust for wealth and power. They will permit, sanction, and order the deaths of thousands and even millions of their countrymen; they come to believe themselves superior to those around them, and that they are possessed of some divine right to exercise authority. In the end, many of them become so thoroughly corrupted by their greed and hunger for power that they are driven to insanity. Some try to take their country down with them when they fall, which indicates the magnitude of their selfishness and arrogance.

Contrast those with this hunger for power with men like George Washington. Washington's greatest adversary was King George III of England, for Washington had led a successful rebellion against the military might of England. According to various accounts, the king asked his American painter, Benjamin West, what Washington would do after winning independence. West replied, "They say he will return to his farm."

"If he does that," the incredulous monarch said, "he will be the greatest man in the world."

Washington, unlike so many before and after him, was a man of integrity. He fulfilled his responsibility to his country and retired to private life. He could have been proclaimed king by a grateful nation, but he only allowed himself to be elected president once the Constitution had been ratified. Again, upon the completion of his second term in office, Washington retired to his farm, one of the greatest men in history.

Washington was a Federalist, a man who believed that a strong central government was essential to the new nation. He knew that the Articles of Confederation had not worked in unifying the various colonies, and he understood the potential of the undeveloped continent. As a Federalist he was joined by John Adams, Alexander Hamilton, and John Marshall, among others. They worked to create the central government they believed was essential. They could hardly imagine that Americans would throw away the freedoms guaranteed to them by the Constitution and "vote themselves benefits from the public treasury." They thought the Constitution had adequate safeguards in place to prevent such things. They were right.

However, almost from day one Congresses, presidents, and Supreme Court justices have circumvented Constitutional checks and balances for their own purposes. Much of what has been created as a result of going around the Constitution is, by definition, unconstitutional. More important, it has created a sea change in public opinion. Americans used to favor personal self-sufficiency under a strictly limited government; today, a majority demands an all-powerful central government that rules every aspect of our lives and provides many different benefits. The natural rights we should revere have been replaced by man-made "rights" with no basis in the Constitution or common sense.

Think about that. How many people do you know who talk about how important it is to do things ourselves? How many of them actually believe that we are responsible for our own conduct and the way we live our lives?

On the other hand, how many people do you know who actively seek government benefits and handouts? When we see someone in distress, how many of us wait for government to help them out instead of being compassionate and charitable ourselves? How many companies have lobbyists in Washington seeking "corporate welfare" or special privileges? What groups do you belong to (AARP is a classic case) that use your money to lobby Congress and the president to obtain benefits and privileges for themselves?

What about these new "rights" and entitlements? When the Congress or the president declares something to be a "right," many people applaud because it will give them something they want that they are unwilling or unable to pay for. These "rights" are usually very appealing; free health care, free housing, free food, free education—the list goes on and on. None of these are natural rights, and none have any place in a free society. Instead, they belong to a totalitarian society whose people are enslaved by those rights. When the state guarantees everything, what the state provides is much less than advertised.

Economics dictate what the state can or cannot do. Any government that attempts to provide benefits and privileges that are uneconomic will ultimately see itself fail. We should be very afraid of living in Stalin's Russia or Mao's China, and yet we are encouraging our elected officials to move us faster and faster in that direction. Free speech is a natural right; politically correct speech replaces free speech. Indecency masquerading as free speech is not free speech; it is an outrageous attempt to twist the law in order to secure a certain privilege.

"I may not agree with what you say, but I will defend to the death your right to say it." That is what free speech is all about. Unfortunately, an uninformed populace has little defense against certain types of speech, like that which promotes hatred and immorality, but to ban it imperils our entire civilization. Rather, we must have citizens who participate in their government who understand and respect the moral values that must undergird our society. Only when we can properly understand the siren songs of those who would oppress us can we keep our government on course and our Constitution enthroned as the law of the land.

## What is a welfare state?

"Democracy and socialism have nothing in common but one word: equality. But notice the difference: while democracy seeks equality in liberty, socialism seeks equality in restraint and servitude."

—*Alexis De Tocqueville*

A welfare state may take many forms, depending on what the leaders have determined is politically expedient. Generally, a welfare state attempts to provide for its citizens from cradle to grave, as we see in some of the Scandinavian countries today. Such a society has declared that all of its citizens will not be allowed to fail. No matter how they choose to live their lives, they will be supported by the government—all at taxpayer expense, of course.

In such a system, people are "free" to lead immoral lives, to ignore their health, to be alcoholics and drug abusers, and to live their lives in defiance of societal norms, all because the state is there to bail them out when they get into trouble. The government will provide an income, health care, education, rehabilitation, and everything a person might need. Unfortunately, this system has never worked for long in any country. Two things happen; those who work and produce rearrange their lives to minimize the amount of taxes they have to pay to support those who are dependent. Tax revenues decline and social welfare costs increase, so that in a short period of time the country finds itself in financial distress.

The people of Rome continued to be fed at the expense of the empire well after Rome was no longer the capitol, but it took the entire Empire to do so. During this time Rome became less and less relevant. The people of Scandinavia have largely turned away from the faith, morality, and integrity that could have made them a great people in the pursuit of their own self-interests. A tour of Copenhagen, for example, reveals one empty church after another, and some of them have been converted into commercial establishments because no one expects them to be used for religious observances in the future. Young people in Scandinavia seem to have little to live for. Because everything is provided for them, they have no reason to strive to accomplish anything worthwhile.

The state has the ability to destroy morality even without actively suppressing religion. Absent morality and ethical conduct we end up with, well, a society like the one we have in America today. We are without a rudder and can be tossed about by every storm. Even when our faith in government is put to the test—as it was after Hurricane Katrina—most of us don't worry about it because it didn't happen to us.

It has long been said that capitalism it the worst form of economic system imaginable -until you compare it to any other. The Constitution guarantees us certain rights to property, and this guarantee enables and empowers American capitalism. There have been abuses throughout the history of capitalism, and you may make the argument that allowing some to create enormous wealth at the expense of those who work for them is predatory and unfair. Nevertheless, when compared with socialism, Communism, traditional monarchy, or any other system of government in which government doles out the economic privileges and punishments, capitalism stands supreme as the most likely to provide more benefits and opportunity to more people.

However, capitalism itself needs restraint when it contemplates environmental destruction, dangerous working conditions, or hazardous products. It also needs to consider conservation rather than consumption for its own sake—but it is not the job of the Constitution to control those kinds of behaviors. Instead, it is the responsibility of society with its mores, ethics, morality, and self-restraint that will or should prevent abuses by capitalists. Just as government can fail to properly represent its constituents, big corporations can lose sight of public responsibility in the pursuit of profits. Men are not angels, especially when profits are involved.

Our welfare state has advanced to the point where illegal aliens receive benefits for which many hard-working Americans are ineligible. It can be very discouraging when a taxpayer finds that his health insurance will not cover a necessary medical procedure for a member of his family, especially when an illegal alien with no health insurance at all receives the same procedure for free.

In this regard the United States has mimicked what happened when East and West Germany were reunified. East Germans immediately became eligible for retirement and disability benefits even though they had contributed nothing to those plans. Hundreds of thousands of East Germans left their homes and traveled to West Germany to enjoy the better lifestyle available there, leaving many towns and villages in the East partially or completely depopulated.

West Germany has incurred enormous expenses in reuniting, and those costs have been paid through much higher taxes on West Germans. It's difficult to understand why any government would treat its own people as second-class citizens while giving full red carpet treatment to a group of people from a different country who have paid nothing for the benefits they receive.

> "Democracy and liberty are not the same. Democracy is little more than mob rule, while liberty refers to the sovereignty of the individual."
> —Walter Williams

There is no liberty in a nation that treats its citizens as subjects.

## Being generous with someone else's money

This false concept is so much a part of American life today that we take it for granted. Because our government does not respect our right to property, which includes the right to the fruit of our labors, Americans are compelled to be generous—an oxymoron if ever there was one.

Americans should always be free to willingly share with others what they have legally obtained for themselves. This is the essence of charity, and Americans are famous for it. It is vitally important that the giver retain control of the gift until it is in the hands of the intended recipient. It is also important that the gift be voluntary. The welfare state reverses all of that. The government forces you to pay taxes, which are specifically earmarked to be redistributed to certain parties unknown to the taxpayer. The taxpayer loses complete control over the money as soon as he mails the tax check. He sees no benefit from the government's use of his money, for it is placed into a large pool of money and distributed in accordance with laws created by Congress.

If the giver can see that his initial gift has produced a beneficial result, he may wish to make a subsequent gift. In the welfare state he has no choice; he will continue to pay taxes because the government will always demand them. The welfare state laws regarding wealth distribution are permanent, regardless of whether the need still exists.

Therefore the giver—the taxpayer—is deprived of any good feelings he might have obtained had he been able to see that his voluntary contribution was having a positive effect. Instead, he may look around him and see the abject failure of every social program ever created and become angry that he is being forced to pay something he finds to be objectionable. Worse, he realizes that the dependencies created by the welfare state will only grow, which means that his tax burden will only increase.

Elected officials absolutely love to give other people's money away, especially when it can buy them votes. In some instances this is called the Robin Hood analogy. Robin Hood was famous for giving to the poor and helping to offset the punishing taxation inflicted upon them by their substitute king. Robin Hood was never generous with his own money; whatever he gave to the poor he had stolen from someone else.

That's exactly what the welfare state is all about; members of the "elite" receive the praise of men and win election after election because they steal money from those who have it and give it to others as a bribe. It's hard to imagine a more corrupt system, but that is exactly what we have in the United States today. The only difference is that in Robin Hood's day a wealthy person could avoid this brazen theft by staying out of Sherwood Forest; Americans have no such opportunity.

Honest, hard-working Americans have every right to be outraged that money is being taken from them to feed, house, and close those who refuse to work. If we refuse to pay, the government will extract it from us by force. No such power or authority is found in the Constitution, nor should it be.

## Social Security = Welfare?

I don't want to, but at this point I need to "step on a few toes." Most Americans today are convinced that Social Security is a government sponsored retirement plan that will provide them with what they will need for the rest of their lives, albeit at a basic survival level rather than in luxury. Franklin Delano Roosevelt spoke of Social Security as being a retirement plan, but he was trying to promote it. In reality, the program is welfare and was always designed as such. It was intended to provide a supplement to the income of retirees so that they would not fall below the poverty line.

The fact that working Americans contribute to the Social Security trust fund is irrelevant; the money you and I have withheld from our paychecks for Social Security taxes is spent the moment it hits the Social Security trust fund. Some of the money is used to pay benefits to current recipients, and the rest is brought out to be used by Congress in thousands of other ways.

Therefore, there are two reasons why Social Security is welfare. First, it was only intended to provide a minimal payment to those who had attained extreme old age. Second, because of the way in which Congress has grossly mismanaged the Social Security trust fund, those who receive Social Security benefits today and those who hope to in the future can only hope and pray that American workers will continue to pay Social Security taxes so that they, the retirees, may receive benefits.

Unfortunately, Social Security is almost bankrupt by the government's definition, and utterly bankrupt by corporate standards. Those trillions of dollars that had been paid in, and which were supposedly earning interest until they were withdrawn, have all been spent and are not coming back.

Medicare is even farther along on the path to bankruptcy. Also, now that many states are in dire financial circumstances, more and more of them will be unable to meet their federally mandated Medicaid obligations.

This is becoming a major concern for Americans. We have become accustomed to Social Security and have been led to believe that it is going to be there for us when we retire or if we become disabled. Our belief in Social Security has been so strong that it has changed our attitude toward savings. Our savings rate as a nation has been in freefall for decades and actually went negative more than once in the last several years. This has made us even more dependent on Social Security than we were before it was created.

When you look at things like Social Security and its supposedly unanticipated consequences like the decline in our national savings rate, and you create a list of other, similar legislation that likewise has produced a negative effect, you begin to wonder how "unintended" those consequences really were. Another example we seldom consider, because it has become a part of daily life, is tax withholding. How many of us would be able to write a check to the IRS every April 15 for the full amount of our income taxes? Very few Americans could do that today. Congress wisely planned for this possibility by requiring employers to withhold income taxes and, later, Social Security and Medicare taxes. Our taxes are due on April 15, yet we pay them year 'round. We receive no interest on the taxes we have paid in advance. The system works, but it is unfair.

There many more examples of ways in which the welfare state restricts our freedom in exchange for a government benefit. During the recent "Cash for Clunkers" program, Americans who signed onto the government's Web site saw a message instructing them that by applying for this program, all the data on their computer became the property of the United States government. Such a statement clearly reflects the thinking of our elected officials, who are happy to give you money they have borrowed or taken from others in exchange for your sensitive personal information. I never heard any commentator mention that cash-strapped taxpayers were forced to pay billions of dollars in taxes so that someone else could buy a new car.

## The appeal of the welfare state

Why would hard-working, common-sense, practical Americans permit and even encourage the rise of the welfare state? That's an easy question to answer. Most of us have an innate desire to be compassionate and charitable; the welfare state satisfies that impulse without our being bothered about it. The welfare state is a great "leveler"; it forces us to be compassionate in accordance with our means. Eventually, it impoverishes everyone. It is far simpler to vote for people who promise to improve our lives by showering us with benefits. Life is more challenging these days, and we all need a little help, don't we? We all want our share. After all, we deserve it.

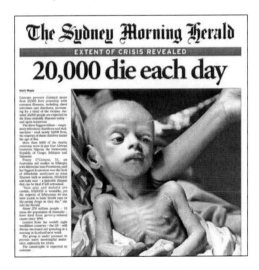

Here are some of the reasons why we want government to be charitable to those we *don't* know:

1. We have an innate desire to be charitable and help those who have less than we do.

2. We understand that there is "strength in numbers," but by ourselves there is little we can do.

3. We believe that all of us ought to share our blessings with others, and we should find a way to make sure that all of us "do our part."

4. We fear that some will be selfish and not share unless they are required to do so.

5. We believe that we live in a wealthy country, and we feel a little guilty that we have so much when so many have so little.

6. We cannot look at a picture like the one above without wanting to do *something*.

7. We are very busy and haven't the time or the inclination to get involved personally. It is quick and easy to write a check but more difficult and time-consuming to be a Big Brother.

8. It's not the fault of the poor that they cannot afford health insurance. After all, they are poor.

9. When we hear stories like those coming out of California about how budget cuts have eliminated treatment and counseling programs for thousands of unfortunate victims, and how those victims would be able to live normal and productive lives if only their benefits were reinstated, we criticize government for failing to perform its duty.

10. "Anyone who says that the government shouldn't care for the poor and needy is selfish and uncaring"—or are they?

Here are some of the reasons why we want government to be charitable to those we *do* know:

1. When we, or someone we know, are in need of an expensive medical procedure or prescription medication, we feel that it ought to be made available to them. We don't care *who* pays for it, but we know *we* can't.

2. We have been conditioned to think that America is a wealthy country and that there is no reason for anyone in America to be homeless or hungry or sick. We believe that since private health insurance is unaffordable to many, the government needs to step in and help.

3. We have been led to believe that health insurance companies are robbers and thieves and that they deliberately set up clauses for pre-existing conditions and other things to prevent hard-working, premium-paying Americans from receiving the benefits they "deserve."

4. Health insurance companies also seem to raise their rates at the most inappropriate times, and recent increases have been as much as 100 to 200 percent in one year. Because we don't understand what is prompting these increases, we feel that they health insurer is simply gouging us. Usually they aren't. Health care costs rise largely because of government interference and bureaucratic red tape; health insurers must pass along their costs or go out of business.

5. Many Americans have not been brought up knowing how to take care of themselves and their health. Our ignorance leads to all sorts of devastating and otherwise preventable diseases. It's considered impolite to lecture family or friends on how they ought to cut down on their smoking or drinking or how they ought to be more careful in avoiding sexually transmitted diseases or how they ought not to overeat all the time. America is the "no-fault" capital of the world; we don't want to be held responsible for our foolish ways. We believe that we ought to have free or at least inexpensive, high-quality health care even for those illnesses we could have prevented by lifestyle changes. Above all, we don't feel it's right that we should have to pay more for health insurance just because we have put ourselves at greater risk.

6. Most importantly, and certainly most compelling, is the feeling almost all of us have that *it's not fair* that some deserving person should not get what they need. We have been conditioned to believe that government can solve everything—why not apply government to solve this as well?

7. We are offered no other choices. The media do not promote free clinics or Shriner's hospitals, or the fact that many pharmaceutical companies give away millions of dollars' worth of product every year. All we are told is that the problem is massive and getting worse, and only the government can hope to solve it. We are never told that just about everything else government has attempted has failed, become corrupted, been co-opted, or actually exacerbated the problem.

These feelings and arguments are compelling. I cannot look at the picture above without feeling great compassion toward those children and wondering if there isn't something I can do to help. The difference between me and many Americans is that if I help, it will be because I voluntarily donate my time, talents, and resources. I won't demand that you donate your time, talents, and resources to assuage my conscience.

That is the great flaw in socialism and in human rights. Under them (and under communism) property rights are attacked or completely invalidated. You are not allowed to own the means of production, whether it be a farm, factory, or even a shop. Next, whatever income you are able to obtain through your efforts is heavily taxed to provide benefits both for the "elite" and for the poor. These are false and dangerous concepts, and they are not part of what America should be about.

Now let's take a look at how bad legislation has helped move us to a welfare state—and beyond.

## CHAPTER SIX

# How Do You Pass a Bad Bill?

Let's take the example of our Congress. It was the intent of the Founding Fathers that all legislation that would be proposed and debated by Congress would support and sustain the principles of the Constitution without favoring any particular group or party. Congress never really worked that way, even in the beginning. Several of the Founders commented in their writing about how the rapid formation of the two-party system severely undercut the ability of Congress to accomplish its goals as put forth in the Constitution.

Today, those who support the Constitution find them-selves in the position of having to fight their elected officials on almost every issue. At every level of government we see one example after another of legislation and decisions that violate the Constitution and often serve to suppress freedom rather than advance it. Many of these actions are not just "Constitu-tion-neutral"; they chip away at the Constitution and treat that document as if it were irrelevant and worthless.

In a criminal court we deal with motive but not with intent. It is not within the power of the court to evaluate and pass judgment upon the thoughts in the mind of the accused when the crime was committed, for we are not mind readers. In our government it is difficult to determine the intent of our judges and elected officials. Instead, we must rely upon their actions and their motives to judge whether they support the Constitution or not. Conspiracy theories abound because of our inability to judge a person's intent. Nevertheless, we *can* and we *must* pass judgment upon those whom we place into positions of power as we examine their actions and discover a pattern.

What we find is that a majority of our elected officials refuse to observe and adhere to their oath of office. In situations where these people have taken an oath to sustain and defend the Constitution of the United States, and the evidence is clear that they have violated that oath, it is the duty of the people of the United States to remove them from office and punish them for what is clearly a crime. Instead, because so few Americans understand the Constitution and have little or no voice in the public debate, those whose actions indicate their disdain for the Constitution are rewarded and reelected so that they may continue and broaden their work to destroy the very document they have sworn to uphold.

If such people were few in number, and if the American people were more devoted to the Constitution, such people would not survive long in public office. They would be impeached, tried, convicted, and booted out. However, when their anti-Constitutional views are proclaimed long and loud throughout the nation by the government, the media, and special interest groups who benefit from destroying the Constitution, our nation has literally committed national suicide, and it will throw itself off the cliff.

> "I wouldn't call it fascism exactly, but a political system nominally controlled by an irresponsible, dumbed-down electorate who are manipulated by dishonest, cynical, controlled mass media that dispense the propaganda of a corrupt political establishment can hardly be described as democracy either."
> -Edward Zehr

As Alexander Pope put it,

Vice is a monster of so frightful mien,
As, to be hated, needs but to be seen;
Yet seen too oft, familiar with her face,
We first endure, then pity, then embrace.

Through the workings of the political process Americans have been forced to endure, then pity, then embrace many causes and ideas that are foreign to the Constitution. Welfare is one; abortion is another. Because we are compelled to embrace these things, over time we begin to accept them if for no other reason than the fact that they have become the law of the land. The government empowers itself to enforce its decision, and we feel it better to submit than to risk the consequences of speaking out.

A perfect example of the way Congress works, even though it shouldn't, is found in the recent debate on national health care. National health care is anything but a new idea; it goes back to the Great Depression but didn't get a strong start until Medicare and Medicaid came along. Here's how the carefully choreographed process unfolded, and how illegal, unconstitutional national health care became the law of the land:

1. President Obama made important promises during his campaign to "reform" the health care system in order to provide benefits for the alleged 45 million Americans who did not have access to health care. Setting aside the fact that this was an entirely false premise, this was the type of thing any congressman or senator who advocated a welfare state would love. Our congressmen seldom if ever speak about the "welfare state", for that is a pejorative term and is better used to attack and criticize a political opponent than to promote a policy or piece of legislation. Instead, they signed onto the high-sounding notion of health care "reform" in order to appear compassionate and caring to those they were elected to

serve. It would, they believed, enable them to obtain the votes of all those who did not have adequate health insurance.

2. All 535 members of Congress and the president need to get reelected. For each of them that is "Job #1"; if they lose the election they lose all their power and authority, and have to accept much higher paying positions as lobbyists. The way to get reelected is to give the people what the people *think* they want. Sometimes that means having to "re-educate" the people and tell them what they want.

3. Many of the American people believe that government is in place to provide them with benefits. They have become convinced that corporations and capitalism are abusive and immoral, and that only government is pure and selfless in its delivery of products and services. When they are offered a choice, Americans have come to know that government will give them the most benefits and exact the least indirect costs for those benefits. Many Americans do not realize how very much they pay in income taxes because they get a refund. Many Americans do not understand that government has no money in and of itself, but only that which it can extract from its citizens. If you can break the link between the cost of the benefit and the receipt of that benefit you can rob Peter to pay Paul as long as Peter does not have the power to prevent the theft.

4. Politicians position themselves as benefactors of the public, even claiming that it is *their* programs that enable people to receive these wonderful benefits. There is much more than deliberate concealment in statements like that; they reflect the tremendous arrogance of those who have been put into elected office and forgotten their sacred oath to defend the Constitution of the United States.

5. Congress and the president engage in an immense PR campaign to sell their idea. They never mention the fact that every similar government program throughout history has been a disastrous failure, or that there is every reason to expect huge cost overruns well beyond any projections made by the Congressional Budget Office. They neglect to mention that their record as the leaders of this country is dismal at best. History clearly demonstrates that when government attempts to solve one problem it usually 1) fails to solve the original problem it, and 2) creates two or more problems of equal or greater magnitude. They focus on the benefits, and the importance of "fixing" something. They do not consider whether they have the Constitutional authority to pass such legislation. Their concern is for themselves and how they will maintain power and influence. They tell us what wonderful things they are doing for us and how vitally important this work is.

The great irony of this process is that in the act of providing benefits to the people our elected officials undercut the very principles that are sworn to uphold. These benefits are being created in violation of the laws governing the nation. No matter how wonderful the benefits may seem, they can only damage or destroy the government and will over time take the economy down as well.

6. Legions of supporters for this new legislation are recruited and sent into the field to pound the message home that those who are standing in the way of this vital legislation must be silenced, or else the American people will not receive these great benefits. The mainstream media and Hollywood are wonderful pawns in the hands of our elected officials, for they are more than happy to promote the socialist agenda since it lines their pockets and promotes their own craft. People in the media would not remain popular for long if they stood up to a popular President.

Have you noticed how interviews are conducted these days? The person being interviewed is treated with kid gloves. No difficult questions are ever asked. Instead, many interviews are staged to advertise and promote the person and the things he or she is trying to put across. Why are there no tough interviewers or tough questions anymore? Because today we have elite who demand that they be treated as if they are better than the rest of us. This is true of celebrities and politicians.

A few years ago I watched a real interview taking place on CNBC between a CNBC talking head and a corporate CEO. The interviewer was trying to get honest answers to tough questions, and the CEO was obviously very uncomfortable. The interviewer was fired shortly thereafter and had to find work at a different network.

7. Special-interest groups that initially pushed for this legislation continue to pour funding into the campaigns of those who support their ideas, while withholding support from those who oppose them. The financial support provided by such lobbyists and groups may be called campaign contributions, but it is nothing more than bribery. The special interest groups portray those who would receive the proposed benefits as victims who are entitled to benefits. In the health care debate the health insurance companies have been labeled as criminals and thieves. No one has mentioned the fact that health insurance companies, like all other companies, are in business to make a profit, and if they do not make a profit they go out of business.

The health insurance companies have been vilified merely for fulfilling their contractual obligations. No employee or employer was forced to purchase their insurance product. The insurance products that are in effect have strict provisions regarding pre-existing conditions, acceptance of new members, covered benefits, and much more. All of these contract provisions are negotiated in advance and approved by the actuarial department of the health insurance company. If not, claims could overwhelm the health insurance provider and put him out of business.

There may be a great deal of greed in American business today, but in the health-insurance industry, where there is great participation by non-profit providers, the likelihood of "evil" insurance companies gouging the public and paying their executives huge salaries and bonuses is remote. Such companies would quickly price themselves out of the market and lose all of their customers.

8. Other resources are often called in to take the heat off the Congress for a time. Court decisions mandating action by the Congress may be handed down, or new interpretations of the Constitution "discovered" in the language of Court decisions and scholarly journals. If members of Congress can point to "experts" who unanimously support the legislation they are working on, it makes their task that much easier. If a majority of evidence does not support the legislation, the truth is suppressed.

9. In the midst of this very private "public" debate about this leading issue, all those in favor of passing this legislation work hard to make sure that the public remains off-balance and confused about the actual state of the legislation in the political process and the actual statistics that supposedly prompted its proposal in the first place. Americans think they are involved in a real debate, whereas our elected officials are acting upon their preconceived notions (and pressure from the special interest groups), and have little or no interest in what the people have to say. Only when the elected officials feel themselves under significant attack from their constituents will they even briefly act as if they have

changed their minds about the legislation. Having done so, and having indicated even momentarily that they are listening to their constituents, they are then free to find a way to be able to say that they had no choice but to vote for the legislation.

10. The legislation goes through numerous iterations in both the House and the Senate. Because it is designed to get its sponsors reelected it must be made very complex, so that seldom if ever will any member of Congress or the president himself actually read and understand the legislation before passing it and signing it. Because the legislation is so complex it can contain all sorts of provisions that will allow amendments and technical corrections in the future. In this way all the worst features of the various proposals can be placed into the bill, and yet the elected officials will be reelected because they can say they didn't know what would happen.

11. Bad legislation can pass both houses of Congress even if the basic piece of legislation itself is not supported by a majority of either house. Just as the special interest groups and lobbyists provide what would otherwise be called bribes to our elected officials, those same officials bribe one another by inserting into the proposed legislation earmarks and other little "carrots," each designed to literally buy the vote of one or more legislators who have stood in opposition. This is one of the worst aspects of representative government, and our nation is not the only one that suffers from it.

12. Former prominent elected officials are drawn into the "debate" if and only if they support it. They serve to supplement the media blitz and all the public statements made by those favoring the legislation. They speak from a unique perspective, for they can portray themselves as being "objective" because they are no longer involved in the political process and therefore have transformed

themselves from politicians into statesmen. In some cases these people are only promoting programs they failed to enact while they were in office, and their objectivity has always been questionable.

As C.S. Lewis put it:

"Of all tyrannies, a tyranny sincerely exercised for the good of its victims may be the most oppressive. It would be better to live under robber barons than under omnipotent moral busybodies. The robber baron's cruelty may sometimes sleep, his cupidity may at some point be satiated; but those who torment us for our own good will torment us without end for they do so with the approval of their own conscience." (from his book, *God in the Dock: Essays on Theology and Ethics*)

13. With all the emphasis on the "importance" of this legislation, and the crisis in which we either are or will find ourselves if we fail to act, the fundamental principles of our government are completely lost or deliberately trampled. A sense of urgency is created by our elected officials and broadcast to the world by the media so that those who stand in the way may be portrayed as evil or hateful or backward or simply blocking progress. Our generation thinks it is the most polarized and acrimonious of any in its political debates, but one need only read the deliberations of the United States Congress or the British Parliament in centuries gone by to realize the debate is no more passionate than it ever was. Only the civility has deteriorated, which is a poor reflection upon those who insist that we must have this legislation.

14. Congress spends millions of taxpayer dollars on TV advertisements in favor of the new bill. The ads are "sponsored" by some organization no one has ever heard of, but the entire program is run by those pushing the bill forward. The advertisements are misleading, inaccurate, and heavily biased in favor of the legislation.

15. The government and the media engage in a policy of "Nacht und Nebel³"—Hitler's famous policy of "night and fog"–to completely disorganize the opposition. It is carefully orchestrated to generate the maximum confusion in order to keep opponents off balance. Congress will ignore its own internal rules when a majority are under pressure to "do something." They will vote on phantom bills that have not been written. They will vote for bills that have been stripped of many objectionable and coercive rules, only to put them back in when they pass a Technical Corrections Act in the next session. They will insert hundreds of pages of text into a bill sitting on a table in the House or Senate without anyone's knowledge, for the bill being voted on is the one on the table, whether anyone has read it or not. They will post-date the bill, so that it does not go into effect for several years. That way they will have moved on to other topics long before they can be held accountable for passing a disastrous bill.

16. At some point in time the Congress passes the bill in its final form and sends it on to the President who, surrounded by acolytes and sycophants, signs the bill with a great flourish and huge fanfare. The president thanks the Congress for all their hard work in bringing this legislation to pass and solving a problem that has troubled the American people for many years. He talks about how he hopes that both parties can work more closely together in the future now that we have gotten this contentious issue put behind us once and for all. He displays his enormous arrogance as he takes credit for making this great step forward for the American people. Only a few people realize what a terrible thing has been thrust upon them, and what a high price they will pay for not having mustered the necessary resources to prevent its passage.

17. The legislation goes into effect and the lies continue. Where we previously saw distorted and incorrect sta-

tistics about how great the need was, now we will see distorted and incorrect statistics about how well the program is working. This will be followed by the various technical corrections acts, which often make the legislation even more detrimental to the people. Since the opposition has been so thoroughly silenced, beaten up, and worn out by their efforts to prevent the passage of the original legislation, they will have little energy to fight these all-important modifications.

18. Having achieved this great victory by moving America farther from its constitutional foundation and closer to a socialist welfare state, our elected officials begin to advance more of their pet projects, many of them even more radical and socialist than national healthcare. After all, they have learned important lessons in how to ignore the Constitution and initiate programs which have brought them ever greater power and influence. The American people have demonstrated inadequate resistance to these programs. It will now be easier to bring about even worse legislation in the future as America rolls downhill with increasing speed toward the abyss.

19. You have to admire the hypocrisy of this process. We elect men and women to public office, expecting them to uphold and defend the Constitution as they have sworn to. Or do we? Do a majority of voters want their elected officials to ignore the Constitution? It would seem that way, because the majority of legislation being passed these days is unconstitutional.

If this legislation is so vital to solve some crisis, whether real or fabricated, why is its enactment being put off for several years?

If this legislation is prompted by a real need which Congress has a Constitutional right to address, why does Congress participate actively in the disinformation campaign?

In an administration that was elected on a platform of greatly increased transparency, why is so much of the business of Congress and the president cloaked in secrecy and conducted behind closed doors?

Why are the American people almost completely excluded from the political process?

James Madison said:

"It will be of little avail to the people that the laws are made by men of their own choice if the laws be so full of them is that they cannot be read, or so incoherent that they cannot be understood."

Most of the legislation being passed by Congress and signed by the president today fails Madison's standards on both counts. Now you know why.

## CHAPTER SEVEN

# What are the Chances of Passing a Constitutional Bill?

How would you go about promoting an important bill that would actually support the principles of the Constitution? How would you gather support? What would you have to do to get a majority of both houses and the president to approve it?

Let's take the example of a bill that might actually require a constitutional amendment. The organization Downsize DC is in agreement with me on several bills I have been proposing for many years. One of them is the "single-purpose law," which basically states that every piece of legislation passed by the Congress must have a single purpose. In contrast, most legislation has a primary purpose, numerous amendments, bits and pieces of unrelated legislation, and certain "bribes" or "earmarks" inserted to sway the vote of each congressman or senator who might contemplate voting against the measure.

For anyone but a politician, the idea of a single-purpose law is a natural one. In fact, most people examining our representative government for the first time might expect that all legislation would be single-purpose. However, our elected officials found out long ago that such legislation would usually face tremendous opposition and would require significant meaningful debate. Even then, it would usually fail because a majority would not support it. Remember, the Constitution itself passed more by miracle than anything else, for those who assembled in Philadelphia were empowered only to revise the existing Articles of Confederation.

For many years I have supported the idea that all legislation should have a single purpose. Of course, conniving politicians can always figure out ways to get around it, just as they can balanced budget amendments and term limits, but *if* such a law existed and *if* an informed electorate held their elected officials to their oath of office, the political landscape would change overnight.

Such a law would probably have to come about through the process of amending the Constitution, which is obviously no easy thing since it has happened only seventeen times in two hundred years. It would be very worthwhile, for it would eliminate much of the bribery that takes place today when our elected officials are promised funds for their state or district if they will change their vote on a particular piece of legislation. A single-purpose bill would not permit that bribery to take place, for each bill would be required to stand or fall on its merits as a single issue. Those voting on it would be held accountable for their vote and would not be able to excuse themselves by stating that there were earmarks in the bill that would benefit their constituents.

Would this solve the problem? Not as long as Americans fail to closely monitor the activities of their legislators. Also, as long as the president keeps issuing Executive Orders and the bureaucracies keep issuing new rules we must obey, the "single issue" idea will not accomplish much even if it is implemented.

Is it possible to pass a Constitutional bill? The answer is yes, as long as that bill is agreed upon by the necessary majorities in the Senate and House. Since, however, our Congress has been working furiously for the past several decades to do things that are clearly unconstitutional, we may safely say that it would be difficult to get them to agree to a constitutional bill. We need to give our term a better definition.

A constitutional bill is one that properly addresses an important issue Congress is empowered and inclined to act upon. That would exclude any bills pertaining to welfare, Social Security, Medicare, Medicaid, the FDIC, the Federal Reserve, bills mandating spending by the states, and many others. Under this definition, a constitutional bill might deal with the laws pertaining to naturalization, the establishment of post offices, the creation of federal courts, or funding our military. Each of these bills is permitted by Article I, Section 8 of the Constitution; however, any bill passed by Congress that pertains strictly to those powers granted to Congress *could* still be an unconstitutional bill.

For example, Congress can attach riders and earmarks to the bill that would enable and fund spending in areas beyond the authority of the Congress. It could take advantage of political maneuvering to grant certain Senators or Congressmen funding under the bill being offered in exchange for their vote. For instance, Congress has thoroughly politicized the debate on immigration. Birthright citizenship, which is proving disastrous to the United States, has little likelihood of being changed by today's Congress. In many instances it is easy to see how the Founding Fathers would resolve a particular issue, but members of Congress today have their own agendas. Those agendas often disagree with or ignore the intentions of the Founding Fathers.

We may conclude that though it is *possible* to pass a constitutional bill, the odds against it are very high. As long as the majority of the electorate cannot distinguish a constitutional bill from any other and do not have an adequate understanding of the Constitution itself, their contact with their elected officials will not be sufficient to induce those officials to pass a constitutional bill—as long as there is a version of the bill more to their personal liking. What our elected officials like is guided by their desire to win reelection and to obtain power and influence for themselves. The corruption that power brings with it is almost always enough to prevent appropriate and constitutional bills from becoming law.

It may not be possible to change the motivations of those in Congress and the White House. The methods of getting around the Constitution have become firmly entrenched, and each new abuse of the Constitution seems to encourage more flagrant abuses.

For example, some of the bills presented to the House and Senate these days are voted upon not only before the members of that body have an opportunity to read them but before the bills are even written. This is a procedural ploy that is gaining popularity because it enables the party in power to literally steamroll the opposition as well as the electorate. It's as if the party in power has decided in advance what it wants to do and doesn't care who stands in its way. They don't care whether a bill is good or bad for the people it will impact; they seem much more concerned about enhancing their own political careers. This is worrisome, for it indicates that the Constitution may be safely ignored from now on because our elected officials are too busy building their own little empires to worry about doing what they are supposed to do.

What are the chances of passing a constitutional bill? These days, it's slim to none.

# Part Three

## What a Constitutional Republic Might Look Like in the Twenty-first Century

"Men fight for liberty and win it with hard knocks. Their children, brought up easy, let it slip away again, poor fools. And their grandchildren are once more slaves."
—D.H. Lawrence, *Classical American Literature*, 1922

## CHAPTER EIGHT

# What Is that Shouldn't Be

I t's time for a couple of important definitions. Let's listen to Timothy Baldwin compare a national system of government with the federal system laid out by the Constitution:

"The national system of government (under which the United States currently operates) is completely contrary to the federal system that our founders and the constitution's ratifiers bequeathed to us ... We the People of the United States of America have been denied our natural and contractual rights under God and the Constitution ... How can freedom exist in a country where we supposedly believe in the 'consent of the governed' when that consent has been usurped by force?

"Make no mistake about this: the U.S. Constitution did not create a national government, but rather created a federal government whereby the states were coequal with the federal government in the exercise and defense of the powers granted to them by the people of each State. The founders and ratifiers of the Constitution expressly rejected the notion that the federal government has supreme sovereignty. The issue here is not whether there are 'national components' of the procedures in the system such as voting for the House of Representatives by the people. We know that the founders implemented a few elements of national-type procedure in the U.S. Constitution, just as they did even in the articles of Confederation.

"Rather, the bottom-line issue is, whether the states have co-equal power to exercise and defend their powers—and their citizens—and whether the federal government has the power to force the states to accept its own interpretation and (de) construction of the Constitution. If the union of the United States was formed by the people of the states in their capacities as the sovereign of each State, creating a Federal government, then the states are co-equal in power and do have the right to exercise and to defend their powers. If the union of the United States was formed by the whole of the people as a mass body politic, without regard to the sovereign states, creating a National government, then the states are mere corporations of the parent company, called the Federal government.

"The founders and ratifiers of the Constitution did not create a nation, but created a federation, and actually expected the states to be the active guardians of freedom for their own people … [4] (emphasis added)

What we have today is a *national* government, one that intrudes into every aspect of our lives and which dictates to the states much of what they will do. Our Federal government has gone so far as to create regional districts through which it may completely usurp the authority of the states and possibly replace state governments with regional governments.

In the northern states today, those that were in the Union during the Civil War, most people believe that Lincoln saved the union by waging war on the southern states that had chosen to break away. Those who grew up in the South usually think differently; they believe any state has the right to remove itself from the Federation of the United States at any time for any reason.

It is obvious that Abraham Lincoln felt that he simply could not permit almost half of the United States to break away and form its own country on his watch. His response to the secession of the Confederate States of America was probably exactly the opposite of what it should have been. If indeed the Founding Fathers created a federal government, as described above, instead of a national government, it was President Lincoln's responsibility to determine why the southern states seceded and to encourage them to rejoin the Union. It is perhaps unfortunate that the southern states chose to fire the first shot of the war when they took Fort Sumter in Charleston Harbor.

President Lincoln did many things during his term of office that made the central government—the national government, as it were—much more powerful. His Emancipation Proclamation was not directed at any of the states currently in the union, but rather at the states that had *seceded* from the union. At the time of the Proclamation, President Lincoln had no authority over those states.

Lincoln imposed martial law in parts of the North, the first time any president had done so. He instituted a military draft, likewise the first time that had been done. He spoke fervently and passionately about the importance of preserving the Union, but in the end all that he did was expand the power of the national government over all of the states. In light of the death and destruction wrought by Union troops during the Civil War, do you think state legislators would think twice today before deciding to secede?

Now let's listen to Forrest McDonald on the same topic:

"The revolutionary state constitutions, however they were framed and adopted, were assumed to be based upon popular consent, and the governments they established, representing the sovereign people, were themselves sovereign in Blackstone's sense of the term. That is to say, the state governments are authorized to exercise any power that was not expressly forbidden to them by the several constitutions. The precise opposite situation pertained in regard to Congress which, before and after the adoption of the Articles of Confederation, had no powers except those that were expressly granted to it.

"When, in 1787, existing constitutional rations became manifestly inadequate, a new compact became necessary, but because of prior commitments, this one would have to be something unprecedented. The Constitution would not be a compact among sovereign states, as was the 1781 Articles of Confederation, nor a Lockean compact between ruler and ruled, nor even a compact of the whole people among themselves. It would be a compact among peoples of different political societies, in their capacities as peoples of the several states. Such a compact was undreamed of in political philosophy.

"Abraham Lincoln thought otherwise. In his message to Congress on July 4, 1861, he insisted that 'Originally some dependent colonies made the Union, and, in turn, the Union threw off their old dependence for them, and made them States…The Union, and not themselves separately, produced their independence and liberty…The Union is older than any of the States, and, in fact, it created them as States.' That view has been supported by some historians, and it is supported by some facts, notably that the Declaration was issued by the Second Continental Congress, that it spoke of Americans as 'one people,' and that in May 1776 Congress passed a resolution urging the colonies to adopt permanent governments.

"But this 'nationalist' interpretation, as it has been called, is untenable.[5]

"Most importantly, the understanding of participants made the plural nature of the events unmistakably clear in the three documents that brought the United States into existence - the Declaration of Independence, the Articles of Confederation, and the 1783 Treaty of Paris in which Britain recognized the independence of each state."[6]

This is extremely important. If Lincoln was correct in his interpretation, the Founding Fathers, perhaps inadvertently, allowed a national government to be created. Lincoln certainly acted upon that premise, as have most of his successors. It is important to understand that the Founding Fathers did everything in their power to ensure that the people of the United

States remained sovereign and that they encouraged their state legislatures to ratify a Constitution that would create a federation of sovereign states. No other interpretation of these documents would prohibit the development of our current welfare state.

It seems obvious that we have a national government today. Understanding that term, and contrasting it with a true federal government, makes for a relatively easy comparison between what we have today and what a true constitutional republic would look like in 2010. Here are some of the things that we have today that would not exist in a true federal government:

- A Supreme Court that has taken upon itself the authority to overrule the decisions of state judges and legislation passed by state legislatures.

- A president who writes law by simply writing Executive Orders, which are given the force of law even though they have not been approved by the Congress.

- A massive, intrusive bureaucracy that invades every aspect of our lives and attempts to regulate almost everything that we do. Most of it is self-sustaining through ever-larger budgets the taxpayers must pay for, and yet they are largely unaccountable to those who put them into power.

- A national retirement program called Social Security in which all Americans who earn money must participate.

- A national Medicare program in which the national government exercises significant control over Americans over 65 and the medical profession in general.

- A national Medicaid program in which the national government compels the individual states to provide medical benefits to people in need.

- A national disability insurance program, which has been made a part of Social Security, under which the national government rations disability benefits while requiring the full participation of all those who earn money.

- Numerous national welfare programs designed to provide benefits to the "poor." According to Martin L. Gross, our national government spends at least $700 billion a year to provide benefits for the 37 million Americans who are defined as poor. If that money were properly used it would totally eliminate poverty in America with many billions left over to reduce the deficit. There are some eighty-five different welfare programs emanating from six different Cabinet agencies, and they are uncoordinated from one agency to the next.[7]

- A national system of taxation which is burdensome, unfair, and wasteful in its administration. Without high-speed computers and very sophisticated software, few Americans would be able to complete their income tax return correctly.

- Millions of Americans who enjoy representation without taxation; unlike the early colonists, who protested taxation without representation, millions of Americans who pay no income taxes are allowed to vote themselves benefits from the public treasury.

- Millions of illegal aliens, most of whom receive substantial benefits from the government and who burden our courts and draw heavily on scarce resources.

- A long history of waste, fraud, corruption, dishonesty, and other serious breaches of public trust by our elected and appointed officials.

- A Congress that can vote itself pay hikes, and which has provided itself with perhaps the most liberal pension plan known to man.

- Government subsidies and corporate welfare granted to powerful minorities and special interest groups that use illegal and legal means to buy influence.

- A National Endowment for the Arts.

- A Department of Education that spends $40 billion each year and has never educated one single child.

The list goes on and on. With an immense national government and accompanying bureaucracy, the poor taxpayers can only hope that at least some of their hard-earned money is being used in a worthwhile cause. Unfortunately, with the immense waste and fraud that permeates the entire system, that hope is a pretty feeble one.

Our current national government is dysfunctional, wasteful, corrupt, and power-hungry. It seeks to dominate and control every aspect of life in America. It engages in massive programs of wealth redistribution, and these will result in the total destruction of the middle class.

Our government is creating a nation of subjects dominated by the wealthy and the political elite. We say we have a two-party political system, but in reality the parties are very difficult to distinguish one from another. Both realize that they must garner votes or die. No court, no Congress, and no president has the power or even the political will to try to stop the pendulum that is moving us ever closer to complete domination by government. In short, the system we have today may well be unsalvageable, because it completely ignores the Constitution.

# CHAPTER NINE ★

## What Isn't that Should Be

I t's time to "think the unthinkable." Americans adapt to the abuse and mistreatment they receive from government. We employ millions of lawyers to help us to escape those portions of the law that will negatively impact our lives or our money. We try to "game the system" and take advantage of thousands of programs to obtain money and benefits from the government. We try to get the rules changed when we can, and comply when we must. As we fall more and more fully under the control of government we have less power to change things. We understand less and less about what might be done to bring about change.

I will be the first to acknowledge that the likelihood of making the change from what we have today to what I'm about to propose has such a low probability as to be almost indistinguishable from zero. That's not what we're concerned about right now. We want to see what we *should* have as opposed to what we *do* have. Once we have the two scenarios side by side, we can make some educated guesses as to the likelihood of making the many necessary changes.

A federal republic based upon the Constitution and the writings of the Founding Fathers should include these attributes:

1. An informed citizenry who actively participate in their government at all levels and who possess a high level of understanding and knowledge of how their government operates.

2. A central federal government that restricts its activities to the eighteen specific powers granted to it in the Constitution.

3. Strong state governments in which appropriate systems of checks and balances are fully functional. State governments handle all the necessary and appropriate functions of government which are not handled by the federal government, and nothing else.

4. A federal government that treats the states as what they really are—sovereign states whose powers are granted unto them by the people through the Constitution.

5. A federal judiciary that is restricted to the Supreme Court and federal courts established by Congress, which deal with cases involving more than one state but not intrastate cases involving individual freedoms. No federal court should have jurisdiction to overturn the legislation of any state.

6. States are free to enact legislation deemed appropriate by their elected officials, who are in much closer contact with the electorate than those at the federal level. Some states, like California, choose to utilize referenda for statewide issues and allow the people direct access; the majority of states choose to utilize their state legislatures to accomplish the same purposes. Each state Supreme Court may exercise the privilege of judicial review on legislation passed by that state legislature.

7. Since there is no national bank or Federal Reserve, the United States Treasury is responsible for the issuance of all currency. In all likelihood, the United States would still be on the gold standard rather than on today's sys-

tem of "fiat" paper money. Fiat money is little more than a license to steal for governments.

8. United States senators are elected by their respective state legislatures, not by the people of each state.

9. The federal government has the power to fund its legal and appropriate operations through some system of revenue generation as described in Article I, section 8. Since the federal government does not have the massive bureaucracies we see today, the cost of government is dramatically reduced and the United States is not a debtor nation. Instead, the United States is one of the wealthiest nations in the world.

10. The American people save a significant portion of their income because they know they will be responsible for themselves once they retire.

11. The American people would be among the most generous people on the face of the earth. Because the citizens of a constitutional republic have the ability to create almost unlimited wealth, private individuals would have the means to perform extensive charitable operations domestically and abroad, with much greater success than similar programs run by government bureaucracies.

12. The American people would be highly educated and highly skilled because it would be up to them to succeed in life - which is as it should be.

13. Americans would enjoy the best healthcare in the world under an open and market-based, competitive system. All medical research would be privately funded, and each state would possess the authority to regulate the healthcare industry and the health insurance industry as it saw fit without interference from the federal government.

14. The United States Patent Office would have a thriving business, much as it does today. Article I, Section 8

specifically authorizes Congress to "promote the Progress of Science and useful Arts, by securing for limited Times to Authors and Inventors the exclusive Right to their respective Writings and Discoveries."

15. The United States Post Office would certainly exist, though in a different form than what we see today. Like the Patent Office, the Post Office is also found in Section 8 of Article I, as are "post Roads." Most schoolchildren are taught that Benjamin Franklin served as the first Postmaster General of the United States. It is interesting that one of the bureaucracies specifically provided for by the Constitution has been "privatized" by Congress.

Those are a few of the highlights of a constitutional republic in 2010. Most of them come directly from the Constitution. Following are some "gray areas":

1. The Federal Deposit Insurance Corporation probably would not exist. If America had retained its gold standard, and if the American people were more honest than they are today, and if the laws on the books were more rigorously enforced, we might not need an FDIC. The FDIC we have today was created in an unsuccessful attempt to get us out of the Great Depression. The unintended consequence of a national system of guarantees on savings has been to make the average American far less careful about where he puts his money.

2. The Food and Drug Administration might exist, though perhaps as a private organization which would be run much more efficiently than the massive and wasteful bureaucracy we have today.

3. The Centers for Disease Control (CDC) would probably not exist, but its functions might be performed by private institutions.

4. The Federal Aviation Administration (FAA) sounds like a good idea, for someone has to perform the essential functions of air traffic control. Should such functions be privatized? The states could certainly form their own organizations.

5. The Internal Revenue Service might exist, though in a much reduced form and with far less power that it wields today. In the absence of taxes on corporations and the much smaller expenditures of a very small federal government, the IRS could probably get along fine at about 2 to 5 percent of its current size.

6. The Federal Emergency Management Agency (FEMA) would not exist. It's functions would be performed by state and local governments. Otherwise the federal government would have the power to engage in wealth redistribution, taking money from one group and giving it to others, such as disaster victims.

This is just a sample. I share these with you because each, like so many bureaucracies created by Congress and the president, seemed to have been established for a good purpose and seemed to meet a compelling need. In reality, few of them perform a function that could not be done as well or better at a different level of government or by private industry. In each case—except possibly for the IRS—their creation would be beyond the power of the Congress of the United States. Rather, that power would belong to the states and to the people.

Think of the benefits that would come from having the states competing with each other to find the best ways to perform these essential functions. If at some point in time a consensus was reached among the states that any particular function should be nationalized, the power to do so could be specifically granted by the states to the Congress, perhaps even through a constitutional amendment. This is completely the opposite of how things work today, and the distinction is an important one.

## CHAPTER TEN

# The Price of Freedom

"It is not the critic who counts; not the man who points out how the strong man stumbles, or where the doer of deeds could have done them better. The credit belongs to the man who is actually in the arena, whose face is marred by dust and sweat and blood, who strives valiantly; who errs and comes short again and again; because there is not effort without error and shortcomings; but who does actually strive to do the deed; who knows the great enthusiasm, the great devotion, who spends himself in a worthy cause, who at the best knows in the end the triumph of high achievement and who at the worst, if he fails, at least he fails while daring greatly. So that his place shall never be with those cold and timid souls who know neither victory nor defeat."
—Theodore Roosevelt

It is not easy to visualize a Constitutional republic in the twenty-first century. All our lives we have been told that America needs to be generous because it can, and that we can eliminate poverty, disease, crime, and all the ills that have ever afflicted society. Well, we tried all of that, and we went broke in the attempt. Unfortunately, the Congress and the White House haven't gotten the news. The media continue to act as if liberals and leftists are rock stars who can do no wrong. They tell us not to look behind the curtain, for everything is just fine and our government will take care of everything.

These are monstrous falsehoods, but they have become the starting point for virtually every political discussion in the United States. We have a president who tells us he will spend money to give Americans the opportunity to obtain a first-time home buyer's credit, and talks as if he was writing a check out of his own pocket. He even has the audacity to tell us that a particular program is already paid for (extension of jobless benefits, November 2009) so that we don't have to worry about where the money is coming from. CNBC, a cheerleader for Wall Street, talks about how "government is going to put money into the game," as if that will fix everything.

What is being deliberately overlooked in this massive hoodwinking of the American people is that every dollar the government spends has to come from somewhere—and you can bet it isn't out of the president's pocket. Americans have become so enamored with government handouts that we can hardly conceive of a world without them. We happily overlook enormous waste, corruption, and fraud as long as we get our check in the mail.

With this tremendous pressure for government to fix everything, the voice of the primary source of funding for all these unconstitutional projects, the American middle class, is being silenced forever. Our elected officials hearken to only three groups: those who pay no income taxes, those who make huge campaign contributions through their lobbyists, and the special interest groups who demand more wealth redistribution. The middle class has no representation, and as a class they are rapidly sliding into the lower class.

Therefore, we have to ask ourselves a question. Should we even think about what the United States could look like if we made an abrupt shift back to the Constitution, since that is an impossible outcome? Or, rather, should we hypothesize a recovering Republic (somewhat like a recovering alcoholic) attempting to repair the ravages of runaway spending and the lust for power?

I believe the latter is the best we can hope for. Even that scenario involves millions of Americans coming to their senses and recognizing the terrible things we have allowed our government to do to us. That will not happen in one year or five, but it could conceivably happen if enough Americans devoted themselves to it for a generation or more. We would have to do two things: 1) halt the dramatic swing away from the Constitution toward socialism and the welfare state, and 2) build a group of Americans who learn to love and respect the Constitution and the thinking that produced it. I want to believe that both can be accomplished.

## Banishing the nightmares

America's rapid decline into socialism is one of the most dramatic shifts in history. We started with the best and freest government the world has ever seen and have tossed out our freedoms, our morality, and our spiritual anchor as we have plunged headlong into the nightmare we have today.

For decades we have seen one dreadful piece of legislation after another get passed, often under cover of darkness, then signed into law by the president. We have seen our presidents issue one unconstitutional Executive Order after another, acting wholly on their own without authority in creating new regulations and bureaucracies. We have witnessed courts at every level illegally mandating legislative changes and forcing their own version of free speech and morality upon us. To any sane viewer of the American scene, this is a nightmare that seems to have no end.

We want to fight these things, but as in a dream when it seems we are running in quicksand, in real life we have no power to influence or change the decisions of our leaders. When they die or retire they are treated as heroes even though they have heavily damaged our Republic and all we should hold dear. Of course, they have garnered fame and fortune to themselves and have the power to shape their own legacy and image to make themselves appear worthy of our adulation.

We have placed judges into seats of power from which it seems they cannot be recalled. We now almost expect them to promote immorality and indecency, and to favor groups who wish to do us harm, and they do not disappoint. They replace parents with the state and claim that parents have no rights over their children. They overturn all the principles of ethics and morality which made this country great. Our judges are falling all over each trying to outdo each other in the race to the bottom, each seeking to do more harm and impose greater government control than the next.

It has been demonstrated time after time that men and women in positions of power are not capable of governing themselves. Likewise, the people's wishes are generally ignored in the selection of judges and political appointees. The party system is a failure, as one party is as corrupt and devoid of ideas as the other. The only thing both major parties agree on is that they will not admit the failure of their actions ever since they decided they knew what was best for us.

Those of us who stand in opposition to these terrible things are instantly labeled as bigots and liars, as traitors and cowards. We are told we are backward in our thinking, that we are guilty of hate crimes, that we are part of a vast right-wing conspiracy (this coming from the genuinely vast *left*-wing conspiracy, of course), and that we are selfish. We are told that we favor the abuses of big business, that we wish to destroy the environment, that we have no compassion, and that we are going against nature by trying to prevent children from engaging in sexual behavior, which the leftists claim is natural and healthy.

In such a world it is no wonder those who love freedom feel confused, off balance, and angry. Those of us who are Christians can become confused in thinking that Christ forgave everything and everyone; he did not. He told sinners to sin no more. Our leaders and the media try to convince us that there is no sin and that there is no God. After all, if God existed, why would he allow_____? (you may fill in the blank)

That is precisely the point. Life is what we make of it. We choose good or evil every day, and we will be held accountable for our choices. Most of those who believe in God have not stood up for their beliefs but have been bullied and cowed by those who claimed that religion was a means of oppression, who told us that any teaching that attempted to proscribe certain behaviors took away men's freedoms. How different would America be today if the decisions of our courts were rendered from the position that there is a God who will hold us accountable?

## CHAPTER ELEVEN

# The Matter of Morality

"Our Constitution was made only for a moral and religious people. It is wholly inadequate to the government of any other."
—John Adams, second president of the United States

"I never believed that there was one code of morality for a public and another for a private man."
—Thomas Jefferson, third president of the United States

I s it possible to restore constitutional government to the United States if the American people and their elected and appointed leaders do not adhere to high moral standards? It may be possible, but it is not likely. If that is the case, what are the chances that the Constitution Party or any other organization can succeed in moving America back to its constitutional foundation? The chances are much better than you might think.

Human nature does not change, but human behavior and group behavior are largely cyclical. We speak of the pendulum moving from side to side, and we talk about making the pendulum move in the opposite direction. As far as human behavior is concerned, the pendulum often seems to move by itself. Civilizations rise and fall; societies pass through phases. Just as there is a business cycle or an economic cycle of "boom" and "bust," there is a natural progression in human society from one stage to the next.

For example, wealth and prosperity tend to lead to pride, loss of faith, greed, and avarice, all of which combine to bring a society down. As a once-great society arises like a phoenix from the ashes of its own destruction, its members tend to be poor, humble, and moral—at least, until they begin to become wealthy once again.

America has been in a great moral decline for at least half a century. Greed, pride, corruption, hedonism, loss of faith, disobedience, disrespect for law, and many other ills permeate our society today. Speaking of Americans as a people and not individually, we have become more selfish and less generous. Things that were not tolerated by society two generations ago are now embraced today. Personal responsibility and accountability have been replaced by the all-consuming quest for power and wealth. We rationalize our behavior, our immorality, our drug abuse, our infidelity, and our perversions by telling ourselves that as long as we are not hurting someone else we are doing no harm. Nothing could be further from the truth.

The focal point of our decline as a people is the removal of God from our hearts and minds and his replacement with something called secular humanism. Now, you and I probably don't wake up in the morning and say to ourselves that we are going to become better practitioners of secular humanism. No, our behavior is much more passive. We permit our entertainment to be sleazy, immoral, and "smaller than life." We accept as a normal part of life the influences of salacious programming, the popularization of substance abuse, the ever-present pornography (which is an offense to all of us), and the "dumbing down" and increasing vulgarity of our public communications.

One of the most important evidences of this decline has to do with the value we place on human life. Now that we have a significant body of knowledge concerning genetics, we understand that less than 2 percent of our DNA separates us from every other animal in this creation. We distort that information to claim that we have all evolved from something less than what we are today. Though man has superior intellectual capacity and abilities over every other living creature, we consider ourselves little better than dumb animals - and act accordingly.

When we legalized abortion, our country, once the greatest hope for freedom in the world, decided that we knew better than God what life is all about. We established an indefensible position about the importance of human life. Once we had given ourselves permission to destroy human life at the earliest possible age, what was there to prevent us from passing judgments about who should be allowed to live at *any* age?

After all, the handicapped, the feeble, the insane, victims of Alzheimer's, those who couldn't "pay their own way" are a burden on society. By logical extension, our society could be more prosperous if we eliminated that burden and terminated those people's lives. In fact, this has been the practice in many nations throughout human history. It had never happened in the United States until Rove v. Wade became the law of the land.

Abortion was not the beginning, however. The movement that grew into Planned Parenthood had been in operation for decades, but it did not operate in a vacuum. Other movements gained a foothold in United States during those decades. It was not too many years ago, for example, that "blue laws" were found in many states and were rigorously enforced. Blue laws were enacted to prevent commercial establishments from opening on Sunday and mandated other behaviors in the interest of maintaining religious and or moral traditions. Their repeal paved the way for other, much more dangerous changes in our laws.

Laws against adultery still remain on the books in some places in the United States, but for many years they have not been enforced. We have to ask ourselves why they were passed in the first place, and the reason that we must come to is that our predecessors felt it was very important to provide a legal framework to help keep society on a moral path.

Another area where our predecessors saw fit to protect themselves and their posterity was homosexuality. Homosexuality was a punishable crime in many countries throughout the world. Sodomy was a punishable offense in the Revolutionary Army. Thomas Jefferson's reformed criminal code for Virginia would have castrated sodomites as well as rapists. Specific language about morality and immorality did not make its way into the Constitution, for the founders knew that only a moral and upright people would be able to maintain a constitutional government. This is not to say that the pendulum was at one end of its path when the Constitution was framed, and it is approaching the opposite extreme today; rather, the founding fathers were trying to set a standard that would enable Americans to enjoy all the blessings of freedom. They knew full well that if America would allow itself to sink into immorality it would fail as a nation, and we would lose our freedoms.

Can we, then, state categorically that because we have allowed ourselves to become immoral and disobedient that we have brought upon ourselves the power-hungry central government we struggle with today? The answer is no. Rather, because we have allowed society to deteriorate in this manner and have not stood up for the principles and ideals our founding fathers held dear, we have permitted our government to seize tremendous power. We cared less about our freedom than we did about our pleasures.

You have to be at least fifty or older today to really appreciate how much American society has changed. Back in the 1960s, for example, a high school student who was sexually active was treated like an outcast and shunned by his or her fellow students. Most of the illegal drugs in use today did not exist. Movies did not need to be rated. Pornography had been effectively suppressed in most jurisdictions, and its promoters had yet to win the many legal battles they have fought since then.

It is hard to judge whether religious observance and belief were a greater influence upon the American people several decades ago than they are today. It is also difficult to make any determinations as to whether people were happier in one period of time as opposed to another. Based on personal experience, I believe that people were better off financially because inflation had not crippled their ability to save for the future. They didn't feel the desperation so many Americans feel today as they run out of money before they run out of month. They were better off morally because they did not have to face the issues with which we are confronted every single day. As far as statistics are concerned, there were fewer divorces, vastly fewer children raised in single-parent families, a much smaller percentage of the population on welfare or in prison, none of the terrible noise that passes for music in our day which can be so damaging to the brain as well as to the ears, less alcoholism, less drug abuse, and less child and spousal abuse. In many households one parent held one job and provided a reasonably good living for the entire family.

Can we add up all of these things and proclaim previous generations happier than ours? The statistics cannot provide an answer, but I believe it is obvious that families in the 1950s and 1960s had a vastly greater chance of being united and happy than families today.

Unfortunately, government was more than willing to step in and help us solve our problems. Today, in part because we have so many "social safety net" programs in place, people do not feel as compelled to live their lives the way they should. In fact, many are encouraged by government to do exactly the opposite of what they should.

A classic example is welfare. If both parents are at home raising their children, the welfare benefits are reduced. If the father abandons his family, the mother and children will receive more money from the government. What a perfect incentive to break up families. This program has been so successful that there are now fourth, fifth, and sixth generations on welfare with no prospect of ever obtaining a decent education and gainful employment.

Of equal concern, the state now feels free to step in and take children away from families for frivolous and unjustified reasons, in the basic belief that parents are generally incompetent and that the state can take better care of their children. This attitude on the part of government can only ruin society. It cannot provide any meaningful benefit.

As Emile Durkheim said,

> "When mores are sufficient, laws are unnecessary; when mores are insufficient, laws are unenforceable."

That single sentence summarizes the ideals of the founding fathers regarding morality and decency better than any other quote I have found. Perhaps no society in human history has ever had "sufficient mores" to make laws unnecessary. Unfortunately, many societies have deteriorated to the unhappy position when the laws were unenforceable. Clearly, America is headed in that direction. We already have a higher percentage of our population in prison than almost any nation in history, yet we fail to prosecute more than 15 or 20 percent of crime, according to some statistics. Several states will offer referenda in this election cycle to legalize marijuana. The laws have simply become unenforceable.

Joseph Smith, Jr., founder of the Church of Jesus Christ of Latter-day Saints, said this:

> "I teach the people correct principles and they govern themselves."

Assuming, then, that the pendulum has swung from its position at the framing of the Constitution to its current position far away, can we reasonably expect it to move back? The answer is clearly yes. Remember that cycle we talked about. We Americans have had our "day in the sun," our period of great wealth and prosperity. We have allowed ourselves to set aside the principles and shed the attributes that got us there, and have replaced them with behaviors and philosophies that are beneath us.

The current economic crisis will help provide the means by which our decline will accelerate. As our hopes fade and our expectations diminish, many of us may find ourselves in very humble circumstances. The transition will be painful, but we can fully expect that our suffering will help us to become better people.

It's a lesson drawn right out of the Old Testament. Only when we have sufficiently humbled ourselves and sought forgiveness will we be able to improve our situation. It will require faith, hard work, honesty, and morality to escape the pit into which we have thrown ourselves. The process is inevitable and inescapable, for we cannot repeal human nature. Likewise, we cannot escape the consequences of our behavior.

Now the question arises as to whether we should do anything to move the pendulum in the opposite direction, or just wait for it to lose the rest of its momentum and begin to move the other way. That is what the Constitution Party should be all about. We believe that because the Constitution was inspired of God, as citizens of this country we have an obligation to defend and preserve it. The Constitution has never been in greater danger than it is today. We may not succeed in reversing or even slowing the pendulum, but we must try. We need to do our best for three reasons:

1. It will be all we can do to prevent the complete destruction of our constitutional form of government.

2. We believe we are fulfilling a sacred calling by defending this inspired document.

3. We share the idealism of the Founding Fathers and believe in the America's potential for greatness beyond what we have seen in the past.

How often in this life do you have an opportunity to participate in something bigger and greater than yourself, something that can provide great and lasting benefit to all mankind? How often do you have an opportunity to serve your fellow men in a way that will benefit both you and them? Can you catch the vision of what this work is all about? Can you see yourself gaining and utilizing talents of which you may currently be unaware?

The task to which we must set ourselves is the restoration of America to its Constitutional foundation. Every American must decide what side he or she is on. One of the things I love about this work is that it requires our best. We must not return evil for evil, but must always be a voice of reason and decency and conscience. A great part of our job is to elevate our neighbors' vision from "the mud below to the stars above." To do that we must first elevate our own vision. As we undergo that process we will find ourselves more compassionate, more caring, and more interested in the well-being of our fellow men.

There are no "victimless crimes." If we commit a so-called "victimless crime" we are the first but usually not the only victim. In a moral society, every individual has a responsibility to himself to proscribe certain inappropriate behaviors, whether they are punishable or not.

How much better would it have been to promote and advocate morality than to legalize abortion? How much better would it have been to portray people as "larger-than-life" than to cheapen and diminish them and encourage us to sink to the level so often portrayed in the media?

This, then, is what we must do:

1. Identify and recruit those who love freedom.

2. Identify and recruit those who can learn to love freedom.

3. Train and educate a large and growing group of Americans who love their country and who are willing to devote their time, talents, and resources to restoring our freedoms and our sacred Constitution.

## CHAPTER TWELVE

# Responsible Citizenship

"We have staked the whole future of American civilization, not upon the power of government, far from it. We have staked the future of all of our political institutions upon the capacity of mankind of self-government; upon the capacity of each and all of us to govern ourselves, to control ourselves, to sustain ourselves according to the Ten Commandments of God."
—Attributed to James Madison, fourth president of the United States

An essential component of a constitutional republic is responsible citizenship. The citizens of the nation must take personal responsibility for their own actions as well as the consequences of those actions. They should live the spirit of the law as well as the letter of the law. We should be well-educated, good neighbors, and do things that will contribute to our society.

Any Eagle Scout should be able to give you a good definition of citizenship and be able to describe the responsibilities we bear as citizens of our constitutional republic. There are very few others who can, and most of them are retired or getting ready to retire. Responsible citizenship is not taught in our public schools or in our universities as it used to be. In its place American children are taught about their "rights" to government benefits.

Citizenship is not merely about voting, nor is it merely about participating in political and civic organizations in your community. Citizenship has to do with gaining a good understanding of the principles upon which your government is supposed to operate, and being able to make appropriate decisions concerning candidates for elective office. It is important for Americans to develop informed opinions about the issues of the day. This knowledge is useful in voting, serving on juries, being a good neighbor, and being involved in making our communities better.

Many Americans hold uninformed opinions and lack the education necessary to contribute to any form of public debate. This would be much less of a problem in a monarchy or other totalitarian state, which require only that their subjects obey the law, not participate in the formation of law. A constitutional republic places a special burden on every citizen to keep him or herself informed. It requires that we conduct an ongoing debate about how we will preserve our liberty from both domestic and external threats. Americans must uphold standards of integrity and morality unlike those under any other government. If we are not good citizens by choice, our republic cannot survive.

The concept of service to country is one that has been twisted and distorted over the years. At times we were told that a military draft was constitutional and gave Americans the opportunity to demonstrate their good citizenship. The draft is not constitutional. Neither is the concept being promoted today of recruiting high school and college students to promote the blessings of the welfare state to their communities. We serve our country because we choose to do so, not because our government mandates our service. We are compassionate and charitable because we choose to do so, not because funds are being forcibly taken from us to provide bureaucratic "charity."

If Americans were to choose not to join the military, America might lose its ability to wage war. That might not be a bad thing if it prevented America from getting involved in an unjust war or a conflict in which it had no business. The defense of American "interests" has never been an adequate justification of military intervention.

On the other hand, Americans have generally been quick to rise to the defense of their country and their liberty, and we might expect them to do so in the future. Just as you can not compel someone to be free, you must not compel someone to fight for something they have no reason to believe in.

Responsible citizenship involves active participation in government. How many key battles has the gay rights movement won in seemingly unimportant places like PTAs and town halls? During those battles, where were the informed citizens who were willing and able to defend their religious beliefs and the importance of morality in securing the blessings of liberty? We were not there; we lost the battle because the opposition was able to change the nature of the discussion. Traditional American beliefs were made to appear biased and "hateful." Each successive victory by those pushing their immoral and unconstitutional agendas made it that much more difficult for Americans to reclaim the moral high ground they had always occupied previously.

"The only thing necessary for the triumph of evil is for good men to do nothing."
—Edmund Burke, Irish politician (1729–1797)

Good people have been rallying and protesting in recent months, as they have finally had enough of the evils our government is heaping upon them. Unfortunately, they are far too late, and the task ahead is much more difficult than it would have been if Americans had been responsible citizens ever since the days of the Founding Fathers.

The same problem exists in the corporate world. Shareholders—those who own stock in the world's companies and corporations—have been more interested in profits than they have been in accountability. A person becomes a shareholder by buying one or more shares of stock, and when he does so he gains the right to exercise one vote per share owned on each issue that comes before the company's annual meeting. Most shareholders are less than diligent in observing the activities of the companies they own. This leaves the corporation's executives relatively free to pursue their own goals. It also opens the door for abuses.

Because of the way corporate law has evolved in the United States, corporate executives are generally not held responsible for their actions. Very seldom do corporate executives go to prison for breaking the law or for lying or other misconduct they engaged in on behalf of their company. Instead, the company or corporation is fined and penalized.

The famous tobacco company settlements a few years ago were a classic case. No one seemed to care that the tobacco companies had been lying and misrepresenting the truth for years about the harmful effects of tobacco use. Instead, the lawyers waged a battle over penalties, for they stood to gain handsomely from major settlements.

In the end, an industry that had been a primary factor in the deaths of almost 50,000 people per year for decades was permitted to continue its highly profitable business without suffering at all. No responsible executives or scientists or public relations people went to prison. Heavy fines and penalties were assessed, but corporations, like governments, have no money except what they receive from their "customers."

The tobacco companies simply arranged to raise the price on their products to pay all the fines and penalties. In other words, future customers of the tobacco companies now have the privilege of paying for the lies and deceit perpetrated by generations of tobacco executives. The stockholders, who generally were innocent (except that they knowingly invested in an industry whose products damaged people's health) suffered somewhat as the stock prices of the various tobacco companies declined for a number of years. The lawyers made millions, and were the only real winners in this landmark legal action. That's how many lawsuits end up in America today.

There are numerous similarities here to what happened to our federal government. Americans were "asleep at the switch" for many years. Americans tend to be good "joiners." We join various causes, often with great intentions, but we are not particularly good at following through. The cause of freedom has never enjoyed a large and active constituency sufficient to overcome all the minorities and special interest groups who were chipping away at our constitutional foundation.

We like to consider ourselves "entrepreneurial" and "independent thinkers." If we really were, the majority of us would not continue to vote the party line as we always have. We have been very innovative in technology, and the freedoms we enjoy in our constitutional republic have made many technological advances possible. These advances have improved our lives in many ways, but they have done little to benefit our society and our culture. America should have produced the world's greatest constitutional philosophers and advocates, people who could teach us how to build upon the foundation of liberty established for us by the Founding Fathers.

It is not too late to "give freedom a chance." Now that many Americans are aware of the heavy-handed way our government is treating us, if we will unite and work together we may cast off the burdens that have been heaped upon us by an increasingly corrupt and repressive federal government.

## CHAPTER THIRTEEN

# Sustaining and Defending the Constitution

"They who can give up essential liberty to obtain a little temporary safety deserve neither liberty nor safety ... "

"Rebellion against tyrants is obedience to God."
—Benjamin Franklin

"The tree of liberty must be refreshed from time to time with the blood of patriots and tyrants."
—Thomas Jefferson

What does it mean to sustain and defend the Constitution of the United States? Every American should know what it means, but few of us actually do. To sustain and defend the Constitution means promoting and advocating its principles in every political debate and discussion. It means making sure that constitutional principles are closely adhered to in every branch and at every level of government. It means holding all appointed judges and all elected officials to a constitutional standard, which includes both the language of the Constitution and the writings of the Founding Fathers. Most of all, to support and defend the Constitution Americans must understand, appreciate, and love the principles put forth by this sacred document.

It was never the intention of the Founding Fathers that America would develop into a two-party system. In fact, they believed that the Constitution would provide a fertile ground for innovative thought as men became accustomed to their newfound freedoms. However, two major political parties were formed almost at the moment the Constitution was ratified, and Thomas Jefferson is credited with starting one of them. In that day, the two parties had to do with Federalism, the belief that America needed a strong and powerful central government, and those advocating the sovereignty and power of the individual states. Almost from the start, the states lost, and Federalism became predominant. It was given a great boost by various presidents, including Abraham Lincoln, Woodrow Wilson, and Franklin D. Roosevelt, along with Lyndon Johnson, and also from key Supreme Court Chief Justices like John Marshall.

Today the Republican Party, the "party of Lincoln," and the Democratic Party are the dominant political parties in America. There are numerous "third" parties, including the Libertarian Party, the Green Party of the United States, and the America First Party. None of these parties fully support the Constitution of the United States. Each has been forced to sacrifice principle in order to win elections or, in the case of the third parties, has considered principles more important than electability.

The American people do not support and defend the Constitution in part because they understand very little about it. Less than twenty years ago the Constitution Party was formed to sustain and defend the Constitution, but these days it is working in a vacuum. Many politically active Americans believe in a "living Constitution," which means it is subject to the whims of those who handle the levers of power. Others believe that the Constitution must include many rights that are more recent inventions if it is to retain any relevance in our "enlightened age." Few people today interpret and understand the Constitution in the light of the Constitution's actual wording and the writings of the Founding Fathers. It is not politically expedient, and doing so often renders a candidate unelectable. Votes are obtained by pandering to various constituencies, not by lecturing them on their failure to understand freedom.

Only a completely constitutional approach can rescue America from becoming a socialist welfare state. That means that Americans must be educated about the original intent and meaning of the Constitution. We need to understand why the direction the country has taken since its ratification is not only unconstitutional but destructive of freedom. Any other approach risks the complete loss of the Constitution. Once we open the door to making major changes in the Constitution to "bring it up to date," we inappropriately open the door to the advocates of socialism and the welfare state. Those people have no interest in most of the Constitution and even less in the Bill of Rights. The question we must ask is, should they take part in the debate on the Constitution since they wish to fundamentally alter it?

This is the dilemma we face. We do not wish to suppress anyone's freedoms, but there are many who desire to do just that. The founding fathers were right to debate the powers that would be granted to the federal government, for they feared that a constitutional government, like any other, would simply seize more and more power.

Do Americans have the right to demand that we return to the original Constitution and restore the freedoms we have lost? Must we listen to those who advocate a socialist government run by self-proclaimed "elites"? I believe the Declaration of Independence is clear on that point:

> "That to secure these Rights, Governments are instituted among Men, deriving their just powers from the consent of the governed, that whenever any form of Government becomes destructive of these Ends, it is the right of the People to alter or abolish it, and to institute new Government, laying its Foundation on such Principles, and organizing its Powers in such Form, as to them shall seem most likely to effect their Safety and Happiness.[8]"

Remember that America did not have the Constitution when Jefferson penned those lines. He was anticipating a government that might be formed if the Thirteen Colonies could overcome and defeat the greatest military force in the world at that time.

My point is that it is the right of the people to alter or abolish any government that has become destructive of the ends described. Clearly, the government of the United States has done just that. We don't need to involve the socialists in the debate to re-establish the Constitution; they are the ones who have trampled it. Instead, it is up to those who love the Constitution to abolish our current government and create a government based upon the principles that will seem most likely to promote our safety and happiness. No government could accomplish that better than the government that adheres to the original Constitution.

Does this mean that a revolution is required to alter or abolish our welfare state? It is the right of the American people to do so, but a violent revolution should not be necessary.

What America needs today is a simple majority who know enough about the Constitution to understand it, who believe in it, and who are willing to work to preserve it. That means that about 150 million Americans need to be taught about the Constitution and the importance of responsible citizenship. Our public debate would be about genuine violations of the spirit of the First Amendment, violations like the claim that pornography is free speech. If we wanted to influence other nations, we would do so from the standpoint of a free and moral people, rather than a corrupt, bankrupt, and subservient one—as we are becoming.

The Constitution is not a "living" document. It is not intended to be modified at will but only through lengthy and soul-searching debate at all levels. Many of the changes we have made through the amendment process have been radical, inappropriate, unnecessary, or counterproductive.

The Constitution is an experiment in government. It is a necessary experiment because no such government has ever existed before, and the Founding Fathers had only imperfect examples from which to draw their ideas. That does not mean that their ideas were incorrect, nor that we should entertain opposing ideas "simply for the sake of argument." To do so is dangerous, and it invites contention and polarization.

The Founding Fathers intended for the principles of the Constitution to be taught in every school throughout the land. They intended for all citizens to be sufficiently knowledgeable to know for themselves whether an idea was constitutional or not.

Because men are not angels, any government like ours in which citizens enjoy an extraordinary level of freedom must be carefully restrained from becoming more powerful. Most of those who run for elective office do so because they seek power. The Founding Fathers hoped that those in the United States who ran for elective office would instead seek to serve.

Americans must be willing to serve not their *government* but their *country*.

## CHAPTER FOURTEEN

# Dismantling the Welfare State

"Most men, after a little freedom, have preferred authority with the consoling assurances and the economy of effort
which it brings."
                    —Walter Lippmann, *A Preface to Morals*, 1929

We now come to perhaps the thorniest question in the entire book. How do we convince Americans that the welfare state will destroy them? If we cannot stop the pendulum in its long swing toward a welfare state, America will soon be officially bankrupt, and shortly thereafter the dollar will lose whatever value it may have left. That is why this work is so urgent. If nothing is done, we will not only lose our Constitution; we will lose our country.

If we could stop the pendulum from swinging any further toward a welfare state, we will still face enormous problems, including the very real possibility of bankruptcy. As it exists today, the numerous government handout programs are fiscally unsustainable, and many already verge on bankruptcy. We are morally bankrupt, as well and show little inclination to restore American values to our society.

It is not enough to simply stop the pendulum where it is today; we must begin to move the pendulum back toward a constitutional republic. Our first goal should be to move America back to its constitutional foundation. Our second goal should be to keep it there.

We have discussed what a constitutional republic would look like in the twenty-first century. Generating the political will to move the pendulum back even a fraction will be a tremendous effort. Unless millions of Americans who are politically involved engage in this work, it simply will not happen.

Two very powerful forces will work against us as we try to restore the Constitution. Our appointed judges and elected officials depend on promising ever more benefits to the people so that they may gain power and be reelected. The overwhelming majority of Americans have become more and more dependent on these benefits, and will fight tooth and nail to retain them and increase them. This is why the Democratic Party has a virtual lock on future elections, as we discussed previously. Unlike the attitudes of many during the Great Depression—when millions of people would rather starve than take a handout from the government—in today's America the majority of people are eager to take more than their fair share of benefits available to them from the government. More and more Americans are trying to get what they can from government while the getting is good, for they sense that the gravy train will not go on forever.

We have discussed Social Security as the "third rail of politics." Any politician who makes any attempt to "reform" Social Security has just destroyed his political career. In the recent debate about national healthcare, most people seemed to be willing to give up some of their Medicare benefits in the forlorn hope that the public option will make up the shortfall. This is robbing Peter to pay Paul, but in this instance Peter is already broke.

Imagine for a moment that you are sixty-five, enrolled in Medicare, and receiving Social Security benefits. You have retired from your full-time occupation and have no plans to work in the future. You hope that your Social Security payments will be adequately indexed to inflation so that your benefits will increase as inflation continues to depreciate the dollar. You also hope that your savings, however meager, will be sufficient to make up any shortfall in the income you need to meet your expenses. You pray that the stock market will not fall further and hand you additional losses on top of those you incurred in 2008.

You feel that you have contributed to Social Security your entire career and that you are entitled to benefits as promised for the rest of your life. You probably don't care that between age sixty-five and seventy you will receive more from Social Security than you ever put in; you will expect further payments as long as you live, and perhaps payments to your surviving spouse when you are gone.

Many Americans who are sixty-five today and on Social Security are largely dependent on Social Security for their living. Those who are sixty-five today are the tail end of a relatively wealthy generation. The next generation, those aged sixty-four and under today, have much less money in savings. They have access to a 401(k) or IRA, rather than the defined benefit pension plan that many current retirees enjoy. This means that they have no guaranteed retirement benefits from their employer. Many of the under-65 crowd have suffered significant losses in their retirement plans, and are seeing their taxes go up and up every single year.

You are probably unwilling to give up any of your Social Security or Medicare benefits. How much less willing will the next generation be when they have saved even less for retirement and can expect to live longer than you will?

Americans are always told that welfare benefits passed into law by Congress were meant to be temporary and serve as a stopgap for people who were momentarily unemployed or in circumstances that prevented them from making a living. Instead, welfare has become institutionalized, and millions of single mothers receive their entire living from government handouts and have little or no hope of improving their circumstances. They have little incentive to seek education and to develop a worthwhile career, and they are bound down by their responsibilities toward their family. Our government has deliberately created a culture of dependence by teaching welfare recipients that they may reasonably expect to be cared for as long as they have a need. How many of them do you think will voluntarily give up their benefits and allow themselves to be thrown out on the street to fend for themselves?

How many farmers do you think will be willing to give up the immense subsidies they receive from various government departments? In some cases they have been subsidized almost since the founding of our Republic. Farmers enjoy protective tariffs, subsidies for specific crops, payments for not farming some of their acres, and much more from the government. How are you going to make the constitutional argument that those benefits are all inappropriate and need to be terminated?

How will you convince universities, trusts, endowments, charities, industry, banking, and thousands of other segments of America to stop taking handouts from the government and put themselves back on to a genuinely competitive footing with each other and with the rest of the world?

Have you searched your situation and identified all the many ways in which you are a beneficiary of government programs? You might want to look at your mortgage or the funding your children have received for their college education or the tax breaks given to your employer or perhaps the Earned Income Credit if your income falls below a certain level. The tentacles of government reach deep into all of our lives. There are thousands of ways in which you can legally pick someone else's pocket; do you know how many of them you may have utilized over the years?

Where will we begin to eliminate government handouts, bailouts, corporate welfare, personal welfare, the massive redistribution of wealth from hard-working taxpayers to greedy corporations and to individuals who refuse to work? The best place to start is always the place that has the weakest constituency. It should also be a place that represents an eyesore on the

American landscape, as some of these massive welfare housing projects do. It could be an area where mandatory compliance violates Americans personal religious beliefs, such as taxpayer-funded abortions. It could be the massive inequalities created by deeming certain organizations "too big to fail," permitting them to gamble with the personal savings of millions of Americans. As we will soon discover, all organizations feeding at the government trough have powerful lobbyists working to keep the benefits flowing. Resistance to any reform movement will be swift, powerful, and nasty.

Where we start is not nearly as important as starting. I know of no campaign underway today that is applying a strategy specifically designed to move us back toward the Constitution in any of the ways I have suggested. What we are seeing is "nullification" and "10th Amendment" movements taken by several of the States in an effort to reassert the authority of the States and the individual against the national government. These movements are essential and should be given our full support.

On the other hand, there are thousands of movements and political activist campaigns in progress today designed to move us *away* from the Constitution. Some, like the gay rights movement, have been extremely successful in their efforts and along the way have sown confusion and created dissension and strife among those who should be standing up to them and speaking with one voice in favor of morality. Instead, we have through our lack of organization enabled and promoted this "tyranny of the minority."

Legislation is vastly easier to pass than it is to repeal.

Court decisions are vastly easier to hand down than they are to reverse.

There is no mechanism at all for reversing Executive Orders.

If you attempt to take people, corporations, institutions, and other groups away from their sheltered dependencies, you can expect rebellion.

Restoring the Constitution is an immense challenge. It becomes more challenging every day as new laws are passed, new judgments handed down, new Executive Orders written, new bureaucracies created, new rules invented by existing bureaucracies, and more and more Americans receive more and more benefits. Human rights have clearly suppressed natural rights.

This is why the Tea Parties and the Campaign for Liberty and the Constitution Party have had so little success. There may be millions of angry Americans, but there are very few who understand the Constitution and actively promote it. We are uneducated, unorganized, opinionated, leaderless, and lacking in vision. If we continue on this way we will never even slow the pendulum as it moves us toward a welfare state.

That said, I believe that enough Americans can become educated and competent to defend the principles of liberty so that we can be successful. It will take time, effort, and money, but in this Internet age we can work much more quickly than ever before. We can reach and recruit Americans by the millions and bring them into an organization that has a viable structure and the ability to take America back. As this organization, which I believe must be a Constitution Party, grows and develops, its leaders will develop the plan by which we will take America back.

I believe the American people will rise to the challenge. We once spoke of the "silent majority." That majority exists, but it no longer enjoys the luxury of remaining silent. We need to examine our own lives and qualify ourselves to participate fully in this great work. We must become patriots. If we do so, we will take America back.

What will you do to regain your freedoms?

# Part IV

## How We Will Get
## from Here to There:
## A Freedom Manual

## ★ CHAPTER FIFTEEN ★

# Restoring the Constitution

"Our country is now taking so steady a course as to show by what road it will pass to destruction, to wit: by consolidation of power first, and then corruption, its necessary consequence."

—Thomas Jefferson

Those words were spoken two centuries ago, but Jefferson was not being prophetic when he made that statement. He was speaking of the events happening at that moment that, he thought, would destroy our new and fragile republic. He was right.

In an earlier chapter I talked about the "perfect storm" of crises that were coming together to complete our journey from a Constitutional Republic to a socialist welfare state. Here are three political aspects of these crises:

1. Our government has been hijacked by Wall Street, corrupt union leaders, socialists, and other special interest groups.

2. The Constitution has been ignored and traveled upon by all three branches of government.

3. Our freedoms are being stolen from us as our republic is replaced by a socialist welfare state.

As I see it, the goal for which we must strive is twofold in nature:

1. Return America to its constitutional foundation

2. Keep it there

In this section I will talk about a hierarchy of Goals, Objectives, Strategies, Plans, and Activities that was taught to me many years ago while I was in graduate school. I will discuss how we may use this hierarchy to lay out a plan for taking America back. My proposed goals are listed above; appropriate objectives, strategies, plans, and activities will follow in this chapter.

What are the obstacles to moving America back to its constitutional foundation?

All three branches of government must share the blame for this crisis.

- Congress has created a massive body of unconstitutional legislation.

- Presidents of the United States, beginning with Martin Van Buren, have written and signed more than 13,519 unconstitutional executive orders going back to 1837.

- The United States Supreme Court and other Federal courts have issued thousands of unconstitutional court decisions. These decisions have wrested power from the Legislature, the president, and the people.

It may seem a bit strange to claim that the Supreme Court can issue unconstitutional decisions, particularly because the Supreme Court has made itself the final authority on what is constitutional and what is not. However, the evidence is clear that the Supreme Court has helped pave the way for our current national government rather than the federal government intended by the Founding Fathers.

Those are obstacles, but they are not the real obstacles. The real obstacles to moving America back toward its constitutional foundation include these:

- America has become a nation of dependents. Most Americans today receive numerous government handouts but are unaware of many of them.

- Our elected officials take money from taxpayers and spend it to obtain power for themselves and get re-elected.

- The prevalent philosophy in the halls of power today is that America must engage in wealth redistribution disguised as institutionalized compassion.

- There is widespread ignorance about freedom and the Constitution. Most of the major media outlets present heavily biased commentary under the guise of news. The vast majority of this commentary is slanted in favor of human rights and away from the Constitution.

The biggest obstacle is this:

- Americans do not speak with one voice when they try to stand up to the government—but the special interest groups do.

Think about the well-organized and highly effective political action groups throughout the history of United States. The list is long and includes the National Education Association (the teachers union), AARP, the National Rifle Association, Wall Street, farmers, the big banks, other unions, the Sierra Club, and many more. Of these, perhaps the most effective has been the gay rights movement. This movement sets a very high standard for organization, funding, unity of purpose, and keeping their members in line. It is for this reason and others that they go from one success to another.

How can we take America back to the Constitution?

## Scenario #1: Fight each proposed piece of bad legislation

This approach is ineffective because of the corrupt means (bribery, coercion, and extortion) employed by Congress and the president in order to pass bad legislation.

> While we are fighting one proposal, Congress will pass others as bad or worse. For example, while millions of Americans were fighting the battle over national healthcare, Congress quietly worked on a massive bureaucratic nightmare of a bill to regulate the financial services industry. It was also working on "Cap and Trade," another monstrous power-grab.

> Once on the books, laws are extremely difficult to repeal. Laws passed without sunset provisions simply go on forever, often long after anyone can remember why the law was passed in the first place.

In a nutshell, the United States Congress uses money it doesn't have to coerce legislatures to vote in favor of unconstitutional programs that the American people cannot afford.

The old adage is, unfortunately, very true: Congress frequently acts to solve problems it has created. In their bungling and politically motivated efforts to solve the "problem," they usually 1) fail to solve the original problem and 2) create two or more problems of equal or greater magnitude.

For proof, just look at the history of disastrous programs like the War on Poverty, the War on Drugs, our welfare system, Medicare, Medicaid, and Social Security.

The War on Poverty, for example, has been such a failure that there are now fifth- and sixth-generation welfare families in America who have no plan in life except to continue living on government handouts. Many of them live in such a way as to maximize the amount of benefit they can receive from the government, which means that families must be broken up and fathers are usually absent from the home.

The War on Drugs has been such a failure that many concerned Americans are advocating surrender and the complete legalization of illegal drugs.

Medicare, Medicaid, and Social Security are all bankrupt under normal accounting standards, and the unfunded liabilities associated with them are large enough that our children and our grandchildren will not be able to pay them off.

## Scenario #2: Protest illegal, unfair, and unconstitutional court decisions at all levels

This approach is patently ineffective, because American citizens have no input into the judicial process. Only a higher court can reverse a judge's decision, or a judge can be impeached or recalled, but there is rarely any constituency for such action.

> When was the last time you saw a judge reversed when he or she "legislated from the bench"?

> When was the last time you saw a judge successfully impeached and removed from office?

There are constitutional means for reversing the Supreme Court, but they are seldom utilized. Constitutional amendments can overturn Supreme Court rulings, but they are extremely difficult to get passed into law.

The recent appointment of Sonia Sotomayor is a perfect example of how people with their own agenda can be elevated to the highest levels of government. Sotomayor is an activist judge who was recently overturned in the very important New Haven firefighters decision. In its opinion on the case, the Supreme Court stated that Sotomayor's decision being based on race at all was a violation of law. So where do we find this woman who was so eager to promote her own agenda that she was willing to break the law? We find her on the Supreme Court.

Robert Bork said it very well in a *Wall Street Journal* op-ed piece several years ago:

> "Consider just a few of the [Supreme] court's accomplishments: The justices have weakened the authority of other institutions, public and private, such as schools, businesses and churches; assisted in sapping the vitality of religion through a transparently false interpretation of the establishment clause; denigrated marriage and family; destroyed taboos about vile language in public; protected as free speech the basest pornography, including computer-simulated child pornography; weakened political parties and permitted prior restraints on political speech, violating the core of the First Amendment's guarantee of freedom of speech; created a right to abortion virtually on demand, invalidating the laws of all 50 states; whittled down capital punishment, on the path, apparently, to abolishing it entirely; mounted a campaign to normalize homosexuality, culminating soon, it seems obvious, in a right to homosexual marriage; permitted discrimination on the basis of race and sex at the expense of white males; and made the criminal justice system needlessly slow and complex, tipping the balance in favor of criminals."
> —Robert H. Bork, *Their Will Be Done*, 10 July 2005

## Scenario #3: Protest unconstitutional Executive Orders

There is no appeal for an Executive Order. Because they are unconstitutional decrees, the Constitution provides no means of removing them.

Even if a president is impeached and removed from office, his removal will not repeal a single Executive Order.

In 2009 a well-intended attempt was made to repeal an Executive Order. H.R. 1228 appeared on February 26, 2009, in the House of Representatives with sixteen sponsors. The bill was written, "To provide that Executive Order 13166 show have no force or effect, and to provide the use of funds for certain purposes."

This type of legislation would, if passed, set an extremely dangerous precedent. It would:

1.  Validate all 13,915+ Executive Orders currently in effect.

2.  Require Congress to pass legislation to counter any and all current and future Executive Orders.

3.  Give the president a free hand in writing future Executive Orders, knowing that Congress believes they have the force of law, and

4.  Give the president powers strictly prohibited by the Constitution.

President Obama wasted no time in writing unconstitutional executive orders. Two days after his inauguration, on January 22, 2009, he wrote and signed Executive Order 13493, which begins as follows:

"By the authority vested in me as President by the Constitution and the laws of the United States of America ... I hereby order as follows ... "

The president of United States has no such authority. This Executive Order, like all the others, is unconstitutional. If either the Congress or the Supreme Court were ever to treat an Executive Order as a legal order, it would provide a major blow to the Constitution.

We must never forget this most infamous of Executive Orders, Presidential Executive Order 6102 dated 5 April, 1933, written and signed by president of the United States Franklin Delano Roosevelt, which included this language:

"Section 2. All persons are hereby required to deliver on or before May 1, 1933, to a Federal Reserve bank or a branch or agency thereof or to any member bank of the Federal Reserve system all gold coin, gold bullion, and gold certificates now owned by them or coming into their ownership on or before April 28, 1933 ... "

Americans were forced to sell virtually all the gold they owned at twenty dollars an ounce. Shortly after the confiscation was complete, the United States government raised the price of gold to thirty-five dollars an ounce. Americans were prohibited from owning gold from 1933 until 1972, when President Richard Nixon "closed the gold window" for the last time and permanently removed any precious metals backing from the currency of the United States.

## Scenario #4: Protest unconstitutional administrative appointments, commissions, and "czars"

This method is ineffective because many presidential appointments are made without the advice or consent of Congress, and there is no Constitutional means of removing the appointees.

## Scenario #5: Protest the intrusion of thousands of government bureaucracies into our lives

This is an exercise in futility, because bureaucracies have a life of their own. At one time they were created by Congress, and in many cases they had been forgotten by Congress. In his book *National Suicide: How Washington Is Destroying the American Dream from A-Z*, Martin L. Gross discusses the tremendous confusion over just exactly how many jobs programs and just exactly how many welfare programs currently exist. The confusion arises because the programs are funded under different Cabinet agencies and different bureaucracies, each created by

Congress one at a time. Bureaucracies frequently overstep their legislated boundaries. In most cases, no legal provision exists to "sunset" them.

There is no appeal or legal recourse from the mandates of an unaccountable bureaucracy. Bureaucracies can literally make up the rules as they go along.

For example, the Environmental Protection Agency (EPA) has promised to step in and impose its own program of "cap and trade" to control $CO_2$ emissions just in case Congress fails to act and pass major "cap and trade" legislation.

## Scenario # 6:. Protest poor and biased reporting by the major media

The major media may look and act like the government's department of propaganda, but they must continue to be allowed to enjoy First Amendment protections. Any other course of action will only destroy the Constitution more quickly.

If we did decide to constrain the media in some way, how do you think it would come out? Would the Fairness Doctrine make its way into law, as so many have feared?

### In other words:

Our federal government has seen fit to ignore, set aside, and abandon the Constitution whenever it suited their purposes. Since their actions are illegal, the only legal "remedy" is to remove them from office.

Removal of elected officials and judges will not repeal a single piece of bad legislation nor overturn a single bad court ruling.

Even if we could remove elected officials and judges who had overstepped their authority or violated their oath of office, where will we find people of integrity to take their place?

Life in America has become extremely politicized and polarized in recent years. It seems like most Americans who get involved politically are merely trying to promote their own agendas and are unconcerned about the Constitution.

# We have been "barking up the wrong tree"

Our elected officials are primarily concerned with seizing more power and getting themselves reelected. The big corporations and special interest groups fund their reelection campaigns and often put them into office in the first place.

Judges appointed for life are not accountable to anyone, which is why they often feel free to base their judgments on their own perverse ideas.

The American people are no longer properly represented in the halls of power. We have been effectively shut out of the political process.

# What can we do?

I have heard it said that because our government at so many levels operates illegally and in violation of the Constitution, the only recourse available to Americans today is civil disobedience. I cannot conceive of a scenario in which civil disobedience or open rebellion would be anything but suicidal for those who would attempt it. In addition, such tactics would only damage the cause of freedom and any hopes we may have for restoring our Constitution.

I do not advocate revolution against the government of the United States. Instead, I advocate educating the people of the United States about the principles of freedom so that they can make an informed decision. We have abandoned our responsibilities as citizens for far too long. Either we will govern ourselves, or we will be enslaved. This is the moment when we must prepare to make that decision.

# The Objectives

Earlier we discussed the two primary goals I propose as being the most vital: return America to its constitutional foundation and keep it there. Now let's take a look at the objectives I propose beneath those goals:

1. Establish and build an organization that will teach, promote, and defend the principles of the Constitution.

2. Show Americans that their current path is leading them to bondage and destruction.

3. Give Americans a recognizable choice between freedom and slavery.

4. Implement a political agenda that will reduce Americans' dependence on government.

5. Lead by example in urging all Americans to abandon immorality, dishonesty, and indecency.

Beneath the objective of establishing and building an organization that will teach, promote, and defend the principles of the Constitution, I propose these strategies, some of which may be just as well be placed under some of the other objectives:

1. Recruit new members constantly.

2. Build a large, well-funded organization of like-minded people who commit themselves to the cause of freedom.

3. Teach members and others about the Constitution and why we must return to it.

4. Train members to lead in the organization, to seek and win elected office, and to stand up to the media and those in government who advocate the socialist agenda.

5. Develop and implement a political agenda that will promote freedom and expose the false hopes and empty promises of others.

6. Wage a constant campaign to expose the unconstitutionality of legislation, bureaucratic regulations, Executive Orders, and judicial decisions.

7. Ensure that the Constitution Party and its platform are constantly in the media—and mentioned favorably.

8. Invite all Americans to participate in this great work. Show them how they may find their own greatness.

9. Demonstrate that a successful political campaign can be fought and won without resorting to the negative tactics of our opponents.

10. Obtain ballot access, and recruit qualified Constitution Party candidates in every election where one candidate is running unopposed.

11. Identify a few vulnerable elected officials who have clearly violated their oath of office by failing to support and defend the Constitution, and institute recall proceedings or bring pressure to bear on the Senate to initiate impeachment for cause.

## Education is the essential component

We cannot defend the Constitution if we do not know it and understand it. We must work every day to increase our knowledge and understanding. Only in this way will we be able to see through what is going on in our government, and recognize what is constitutional and what is not.

Without a solid foundation in the Constitution, we cannot stand up to those who proclaim that the Constitution is a "living" document. We cannot explain why the Constitution was intended to prohibit wealth redistribution.

If we do not gain a firm understanding of the Constitution and teach our children adequately, any progress we may make in our lifetime will be thrown away by the next generation. Each generation must gain its own appreciation for freedom and fight for it, or it will disappear.

Thomas Jefferson said:

"Educate and inform the whole mass of the people ... They are the only sure reliance for the preservation of our liberty."

George Washington said:

"A primary object should be the education of our youth in the science of government. In a republic, what species of knowledge can be equally important? And what duty more pressing ... than ... communicating it to those who are to be the future guardians of the liberties of the country?"

We are very busy people. Our time is tied up in family, work, hobbies, TV, friends, video games, and much more. I think that most of us can find some time in our busy schedules to study and learn about the Constitution.

Many who consider themselves conservatives spend a lot of time reading "problem" books like *Liberty and Tyranny* by Mark Levin and *National Suicide* by Martin Gross. We also spend a lot of time watching or listening to Sean Hannity, Glenn Beck, and Rush Limbaugh. May I suggest as gently as possible that your knowledge of the Constitution is not going to increase by engaging in any of these activities? If you want to learn about the Constitution, the best place to start is the Constitution itself. After that, you should read books specifically written about the Constitution by people who loved and respected it. *The 5,000 Year Leap* comes to mind, as well as many of the publications available from the National Center for Constitutional Studies (NCCS).

I believe many conservatives are not using their time wisely when they get wrapped up in conspiracy theories, headlines and in "who said what to whom." On those few occasions when I have listened to conservative talk radio I have turned it off after a few minutes, because nothing was being accomplished. Spending an hour or two talking about what some Senator said in an unguarded moment will not help to move America back to its constitutional foundation. In fact, most of what I hear and see in the media these days on both sides is misleading and counterproductive as well as useless, often bordering on gossip.

It may be fun to catch people we don't like in moments when they make mistakes, but spending hours and hours pointing out those mistakes makes us look even worse. We love entertainment, and we are thrilled to hear or see something put together by people who are "on our side," but if it does not educate us it is usually a waste of our time.

I recently tuned in to the Fox TV network for the first time. I had heard much about how it was a conservative alternative to the very liberal National Public Radio (NPR) and all of the liberal media. What I saw was heavily biased reporting, gross misstatements, politicized news stories, and the same kind of gossip and finger-pointing I had heard on NPR.

It is obvious that the liberal media are heavily biased in favor of socialism and the welfare state, and that is what we would expect from the party of empty promises. What I had hoped for on the other side was honesty and integrity in reporting, but I have yet to find it. Do people really believe that two wrongs make a right?

There is something else about being independent and having our own opinions. Having a two-party political system almost eliminates the need for conscious thought. If you are a Democrat, and have voted for the Democratic Party your entire life, it's easy to pull that single lever that will cast your ballot on behalf of all the Democratic Party candidates on the ticket. Millions of Americans today do just exactly that; neither Democrats nor Republicans need to exercise their brains when they pull that lever. The two-party system fails completely when both parties feel free to ignore the Constitution.

Belonging to a Tea Party requires more thought, and many people seem to find it uncomfortable. I have spoken with a few people who turned out to protest something, and when they were challenged by someone on the opposite side of the issue found that their knowledge and understanding was inadequate. Most of them were embarrassed at having been incapable of refuting even the simplest of the liberal or socialist arguments.

Many of us are also ignorant of the facts, and absent a factual background we are easily put in our place by half truths and untruths. That's not entirely our fault, however; the liberal dominance of all the media, the public schools, the universities, and Washington for so many decades has made it very difficult for truth to come forth.

We have been complacent for far too long, and we have let our standards slide concerning education and citizenship. I have seen differences of opinion vented at numerous political events, and in many cases the differences remain unresolved because no one could speak with authority and expertise. We cannot argue from our ignorance, nor can we argue from our own unique point of view.

Alexis de Tocqueville said this:

> "If each undertook himself to form all his opinions and to pursue the truth in isolation down paths cleared by him alone, it is not probable that a great number of men would ever unite in any common belief...without common ideas there is no common action, and without common action men still exist, but a social body does not."

We need a "social body" oriented around the Constitution, an organization full of people who love and respect the Constitution and who want to apply its principles today. As we become better educated, we will begin to shed our uninformed opinions, which will make us more capable of responding intelligently to the issues of the day. However, if our *informed* opinions still divide us, we will accomplish nothing because we will remain in isolation one from another. As Thoreau said:

> "For every thousand hacking at the leaves of evil, there is one striking at the root."

The Tea Parties, the Libertarian Party, the 9/12 Movement, the Campaign for Liberty, and hundreds of other organizations across United States are all "hacking at the leaves of evil," but if we could unite we could strike at the root. To do that, we must understand the enemy. The enemy, as we have defined previously, is the rapid progress of human rights and the way their implementation is destroying governments and economies.

It is not enough to understand, respect, and even revere the Constitution; we must also find effective ways to teach self-reliance, self-discipline, and self-government. Human rights will always appeal to the less educated. We can only hope that those with more education will seek to improve themselves, rather than seeking to become the elite who rule over those who believe in human rights.

## CHAPTER SIXTEEN

# Changing the Political Landscape

How do you go about moving America away from a socialist welfare state and back toward a constitutional republic? It is not enough to state the problem, as so many well-known authors and commentators have done. It is essential that we know what we are about. Very few Americans have any idea of the nature of the problems we face, much less how we can go about solving those problems. There are perhaps as many conservative political movements alive in America today as there are religious faiths, which is one reason why our government has become so big and has gone so far astray.

We are not united as Americans who demand that our Constitution be respected, heeded, and obeyed. Many of us get all wrapped up in "conspiracy theories" or engage in activities that on the surface may seem to be giving us an outlet to express our grievances, but most of them simply waste our time and prevent us from becoming united in a vital common cause.

The challenge we face as Americans who love liberty and wish to defend our constitutional republic is that the Constitution today has almost no constituency. During the first few years following the ratification of the Constitution, all three branches of government were primarily concerned with whether something was constitutional or not. We had the Federalist party and the Anti-Federalist Party, the one promoting a strong central government and the other focusing primarily on states' rights.

Today the situation is very different. In most of our political debate and in many of our courts all the way up to the Supreme Court, the question is not whether something is constitutional but rather whether it is politically expedient. Our leaders seem determined to make steadfast progress toward the fulfillment of a particular agenda far removed from what America should be. In a constitutional republic that has two major political parties, those parties should be Federalist and Anti-Federalist, and the debate should focus on the constitutionality of each issue. How will we move back toward that particular method of operation?

## Can we "reform" the Republican or Democratic Parties?

Most Americans who vote Democratic tend to think that we just need to take more money from the taxpayers and throw it at the problems liberals have failed to solve over the past 150 years. Most Americans who vote Republican tend to think that we just need to get the Republican party back to its conservative base. Both views are wrong. Neither major party today is particularly concerned with what the Constitution says, and as a result both have turned their attention toward getting votes and holding onto power. It seems as if at the same time they have been discarding the Constitution they have also been discarding their ethical and moral standards.

"Reforming" a political party, if it were possible, involves several steps:

1. Change the way Party members think about the issues.

2. Change the Party's platform to one focused on the Constitution.

3. Change the political processes under
   which the Party functions.

Such things are accomplished over a generation or longer, and they only happen if those in power want it to happen. I have very little confidence that we can get the major parties to change their ways. After all, they deliberately created our current mess and have profited from it. Why should they change? Even if you could accomplish these three things, you must still complete the original task of *Restoring the Constitution*.

How would you go about changing the way members of the Republican Party think about the issues?

1. Teach them about the Constitution and
   the writings of the Founding Fathers.

2. Teach them about integrity, morality,
   decency, and fair play.

3. Teach them about properly representing
   the people they are supposed to serve.

4. Undo all of their experience in
   trampling the Constitution in order to
   get reelected and to gain power.

5. Break the connections between Party members and
   special interest groups, Wall Street, and big business.

If only one of the two dominant political parties were to restructure itself and focus on the Constitution, in today's political climate they would never again be able to win an election.

## In Defense of the Tea Parties

The Tea Party Movement has capitalized on the anger many Americans are feeling as our government stumbles blindly through this massive economic crisis and wastes trillions of taxpayer dollars bailing out financial institutions that caused most of the problems in the first place. Some of the Tea Party groups have become effective in political activism and can claim some credit in slowing the progress of certain legislation through Congress. However, because of the ways in which the laws hamstring these organizations, none of these conservative movements can move the pendulum back toward the Constitution and away from the welfare state. Their agenda must stop short of doing many other things that absolutely must be done.

Only a political party can engage in all of the activities that must be undertaken, and no political party has ever attempted to do all that I propose in the pages that follow.

## The Constitution Party

We need to update our definitions of political parties. We all have a pretty good idea of what political parties do. Many of us rely on our political party affiliation to tell us how we should vote and the point of view we ought to take when we talk about things with our friends, neighbors, and associates.

A political party by virtue of its structure enjoys a certain freedom of action not available to any other type of organization. A political party can gain ballot access and can actually endorse and run candidates for elective office.

There is a political party United States today that is struggling to make itself known. It is called the Constitution Party, and it is not making great progress. Here's how I see the Constitution Party as it should exist today.

## A Different Kind of Political Party

I propose that we use a political party whose platform is based on the original Constitution to engage in all the appropriate activities common to political parties as we know them today, and also to engage in activities we wouldn't normally associate with a political party.

For example, we don't think of political parties as being educational institutions that focus on making sure that all of their members have a thorough and complete understanding of the principles of government or even the principles of the Party.

This party will do just that. This Constitution Party needs to create its own constituency, for most Americans know very little about the Constitution and what is constitutional and what is not. Most Americans cannot distinguish between an inalienable right and a "right" that permits us to pick someone else's pocket. This knowledge is essential and it must become as widespread as possible if we are to be able to move America back toward its constitutional foundation.

This educational approach may sound simplistic and unrealistic, but it is not. Think of it this way: There are hundreds of ways we can attempt to slow or stop the things our government is doing to us, but only a few people have the knowledge and training to know what can be done and how to do it. The first thing they must do is convince others that their plan is worthwhile. They must build a constituency for their ideas, rally support, raise money, hire attorneys and lobbyists, plan and organize political action activities, and build an entire organization around that particular idea. This will expend the relatively scarce resources of conservatives on a project that may not be as good as something someone else has proposed.

Whether it is successful or not, once this plan has been completed the constituency will disintegrate. Each member will follow after another cause or drop out of conservative political action altogether for a time. This is one reason why political action groups like the Citizens against Government Waste (CAGW), Judicial Watch, and the Heritage Foundation want you to become a member of their organization and make regular contributions. Their agendas are mostly reactive, and they have no specific plan by which they will move America back to its constitutional foundation because they do not have that vision or that goal.

Now compare that with the gay-rights movement. People at the top of that movement have made all the critical decisions as to which battles they will create, the specific resources and dollars and manpower allocated to that battle, the slate of events that will be conducted in order to win the battle, and so on. Win or lose, once the battle is over, supporters of the gay-rights movement will still be active supporters of the gay-rights movement and will be involved in the next battle because they know the complete agenda and have signed on for the long haul.

It is this type of commitment that the Constitution Party can create. As the Constitution Party recruits, educates, and trains its members, Party leaders at all levels will work together to lay out a complete agenda with which we can proactively move America back to its constitutional foundation. We will decide (we meaning Party members and leaders) what battles are to be fought, rather than simply reacting to the news of the day as most conservative organizations do. Members of the party will sign on to the plan and know exactly what is expected of them if we are to be able to win each battle.

The Constitution Party will become a large and growing group of well-educated Americans who understand the Constitution and who love liberty. We will understand the ways in which America has strayed from the Constitution, and commit ourselves to a detailed agenda by which we hope to restore America to its constitutional foundation.

The educational approach is only one aspect of what this political party will do. This party will actively engage in recruiting and educating Americans at the grassroots level so that they may become actively and effectively involved in restoring our freedoms. It will bring to the public's attention constitutional alternatives to the issues of the day and will assist our elected officials by giving them an appropriate alternative to the things they are being pressured to do. It will engage the media to promote the messages of freedom and liberty and self-reliance. These themes will touch many hearts and help turn anger into commitment.

This party will bring decency, integrity, and morality back into the public debate, otherwise those attributes would be absent. This party will show America that there is a better and higher way in which to conduct the affairs of government for the benefit—the "general welfare"—of all Americans, not just those who make the most noise or throw the most money at reelection campaigns.

This party will obtain ballot access wherever possible and run suitable, well-qualified candidates in as many races as it can. In each instance these candidates will promote not their own personal agenda but the agenda of the Constitution.

This party will build itself into an effective force for good at the grassroots level and also at the state and national levels. I do not foresee that this party will have any effect on national races for years to come, for at present it is seriously underfunded and has a very small constituency. This party also enjoys very little name recognition, and today is not even called the Constitution Party in all fifty states.

## A "third party"?

This party—this *Constitution* Party—will not look much like a typical third party. Surely it will not be able to buy its way into a presidential election the way Ross Perot did and will seldom serve as a "spoiler" to the plans of the Republican Party. Constitution Party members serving in elected office will in many instances side with the Republicans, as long as the Republicans are either following the Constitution or at least promoting conservative principles.

Politics is about power-sharing and consensus. Nothing—including the framing and ratification of the Constitution—is accomplished if a group or party demands that things be done their way and only their way. That's why it is so vitally important that we begin from a position of strength, rather than one of weakness.

The Constitution Party elected officials may, on occasion, side with the Democrats when the Republicans are anxiously soliciting the support of Wall Street and big business in exchange for more and more corporate welfare. Those elected as Constitution Party candidates will use their authority and influence to try to change the political debate away from bringing more power and money to Washington, and toward the principles of liberty under which this country was founded.

There are many possible outcomes springing from the successful rise to prominence of a well-organized, disciplined Constitution Party. Once the Constitution Party attains "critical mass" and is capable of influencing the outcome of national elections and the public debate on major issues, in theory the Constitution Party could become a true "third-party" and might be a "spoiler" in some Congressional and Presidential elections. It is my hope that by that time the leaders of both the Democratic and Republican parties will have found some reason to begin considering the Constitution once again. Both can comfortably ignore it today because of the widespread ignorance of and apathy about the Constitution, but the Constitution Party will change all that.

Do we need to fear that the Constitution Party will "give" a presidential election to the Democrats to because it draws away enough conservatives from the Republican camp? It is a possibility, but a small one. Instead, I anticipate that the Republicans may actually recruit a presidential or vice presidential candidate from the Constitution Party, which would give them a much better chance of winning.

I believe that millions of Americans will respond favorably to a political party that offers unbiased education about the Constitution and the issues of the day, a party that does not attack its opponents but instead attempts to find common, constitutional ground with them on the important issues.

One of the most important things the Constitution Party can do is to awaken millions of Americans to an understanding of their responsibility as citizens of this great Republic. If we are knowledgeable, credible, and sufficiently numerous, our elected officials and the media will simply have to listen to us.

There are many issues facing America today that are simply not addressed by the Constitution. We must debate and decide upon these issues, and we would be vastly better off if the debate would begin with the Constitution rather than the basic tenets of government as we have them today. It's not just the Constitution that matters; it's the morality, decency, and integrity of the American people that must be considered in deciding each of these issues. In that sense, the work of the Constitution Party also involves promoting morality throughout the land, which is why it is so vitally important that we lead by example.

## The Constitution Party I propose:

1. The Party will incorporate into its mission statement two primary goals;

   - Return America to its constitutional foundation, and
   - Keep it there

2. The Party will actively and constantly recruit new members by educating the public about the Constitution and asking Americans to take part in achieving these goals.

3. The Party will train tens of thousands of Americans to serve in the Party and to run for, win, and serve in elective office.

4. The Party will continue to seek and obtain ballot access in all 50 states.

5. The Party will run well-qualified candidates in thousands of elections at every level. Candidates will be held to the high standards imposed upon them by the Party platform and by the requirements placed upon all Party members.

This is much more than just a political party; this is a movement to bring back something we have lost, something very precious. You may think it easy to dismiss these things as idealistic or wishful thinking or just plain impossible. What was impossible was the framing of the Constitution itself, and yet it was accomplished. We face tremendous resistance in moving away from the welfare state, and yet it can be done if you and millions of other Americans will do your part.

## CHAPTER SEVENTEEN

# Setting the Stage

I t is certainly time to try new methods to eliminate the divisiveness, deceit, hypocrisy, and double dealing of American politics today. What we have seen so far has only polarized Americans and caused us to focus on things that have little or no real value in the political debate. If the Constitution Party merely duplicates the efforts of its conservative peers, it will accomplish little or nothing. We need a new approach.

The only way to save our republic is for men and women of faith and conscience to unite under the banner of freedom. We must create a political organization that will rally Americans around the Constitution and help them gain for themselves the desire to reestablish it as the law of the land and the foundation of a just and moral government.

To date our efforts have been too little and too ineffective. That must change. A thousand separate groups proclaiming the Constitution simply cannot be effective. When the media play the story about Tea Party protestors likening Obama to Hitler, we gain no credibility and no influence.

The Constitution Party must be revitalized with the time and talents of millions of new members, all of whom have made a commitment to serve regularly and diligently. They must be educated so that they have a thorough understanding of the Constitution. They must be trained to participate in the political process and to invite and recruit others. They must learn to work together in a common cause. The leaders of the Constitution Party must identify the unique talents and abilities of each member so that they may be put to good use in restoring the Constitution.

What sort of people will bring America back? They will come from every race, every income bracket, every religion, every political philosophy, and every walk of life. Many will have never served a cause before, and doing so will be new to them. All should become better men and women through their involvement with this great work. Not only will they become more knowledgeable and better-informed citizens; they will improve their lives through their active involvement in the cause of freedom.

Twenty-four hundred years ago, the great Athenian general Thucydides delivered a famous funeral oration in which he talked about the kind of man who offered up his life for his country:

> "For there is justice in the claim that steadfastness in his country's battles should be as a cloak to cover a man's other imperfections; since the good action has blotted out the bad, and his merit as a citizen more than outweighed his demerits as an individual.

> "But none of these allowed either wealth with its prospect of future enjoyment to unnerve his spirit, or poverty with its hope of a day of freedom and riches to tempt him to shrink from danger. No, holding that vengeance upon their enemies was more to be desired than any personal blessings, and reckoning this to be the most glorious of hazards, they joyfully determined to accept the risk, to make sure of their vengeance, and to let their wishes wait; and while committing to hope the uncertainty of final success, in the business before them they thought fit to act boldly and trust in themselves. Thus choosing to die resisting, rather than to live submitting, they fled only from dishonour, but met danger face to face, and after one brief moment, while at the summit of their fortune, escaped, not from their fear, but from their glory."

In other words, though these men who died for Greece had their faults and imperfections, as we all do, in devoting and ultimately in giving their lives for something greater than themselves they set an example for all who love freedom. Thucydides addresses the survivors of the great battle and the families of the fallen:

> "So died these men as became Athenians. You, their survivors, must determine to have as unfaltering a resolution in the field, though you may pray that it may have a happier issue. And not contented with ideas derived only from words of the advantages which are bound up with the defense of your country … you must yourselves realize the power of Athens, and feed your eyes upon her from day to day, till love of her fills your hearts; and then, when all her greatness shall break upon you, you must reflect that it was by courage, sense of duty, and a keen feeling of honour in action that men were enabled to win all this, and that no personal failure in an enterprise could make them consent to deprive their country of their valour, but they laid it at her feet as the most glorious contribution that they could offer."

You might ask yourself whether anyone could feel that way today about their country or about freedom or about anything else. My answer is that all of us can if we are invited to do so and if we can catch the vision of what we may bring to pass. We need to be much more than flag-wavers; we need to stand up for what is right and restore hope in every American heart. We can only do so if we comprehend the value of the freedom others are discarding.

We need to build a group of people who know what freedom is and are willing to work for it. It will mean sacrifice, hard work, and all that is good in us. We will experience discouragement, frustration, humiliation, and even occasional defeat. In the end, no matter the ultimate outcome, we will have given our time, talents, and resources in the service of a cause next to godliness. We will have clothed ourselves with respect for all men, compassion, virtue, and charity as we have labored to make all Americans free.

Are we up to the task? Can we succeed? We are, and we can, if we are united. We must overcome petty differences. We must stay away from partisan wrangling. We must be exemplary in our conduct, for we seek to attract to our cause people who live that way themselves.

We must not allow ourselves to sink to the level of today's selfish grasping for power. We seek to free men, not to bind them to false hopes and empty promises.

We are late to the battle. We have allowed Americans to lose their understanding of the Constitution and we have not required that our children be taught its principles. Our only hope is in helping Americans believe in freedom once again so that they will work for it. If we are content to sit in the recliner with a beer and the remote, we will fail.

## Walking a Tightrope

We are walking a tightrope. If we preach the Constitution as it was originally drafted—and much of our effort will be in that context—we will be attacked for being out-of-date, behind the times, uninformed, and incapable of dealing with the world today. Certainly we will be attacked for taking any position that does not fully endorse human rights. None of this criticism will be appropriate, but it is the way politics is conducted, and it will do damage. We will be attacked on the basis that the Constitution is a "living" document, one that must be changed to meet the needs of the people in our day. If we continue to press for the "strict construction" argument, the response will be to do away with the Constitution altogether. This we simply cannot afford. We are already headed in that direction because there are many who want our government to be dissolved into a "one world" government. We are under ever-greater pressure to abandon our sovereignty and submit to the unelected "government" of the world's elites.

We cannot afford to allow ourselves to be isolated and marginalized by those who have the loudest voices and the greatest influence. We also cannot passively stand by, signing petitions and attending Tea Parties. We must be actively involved in defending our Constitution.

We are also walking a different kind of tightrope. There are many Americans who believe in a version of the Constitution different from the one we currently have. I refer to the Libertarians, those who believe that the Constitution guarantees them the freedom to engage in any activity that does not harm someone else. The Libertarian approach, as I understand it, is basically amoral in that it does not take a stand on issues like homosexuality, abortion, and illegal drugs. However, when confronted with those issues, the Libertarian fallback position seems to permit all those behaviors—both legal and illegal—because of their definition of victimless crimes.

This approach is very dangerous to the Constitution. I believe that many Libertarians will not support a "strict construction" approach to the Constitution because they 1) believe in rights in addition to natural rights, 2) do not have morality as the underlying principle of their beliefs, and 3) are willing to "go with the flow" on many issues instead of standing up for important principles.

I want to believe that many Libertarians will join with us in our efforts because they actually do support the principles of morality and decency, but they must be sought out and recruited. We cannot expect their help unless they are willing to abandon Libertarianism and cleave to the Constitution itself. If they will not, we may find them abandoning us at key moments.

## Education

We need to proceed on multiple levels simultaneously:

1. Educate ourselves regarding the principles of freedom, the Declaration of Independence, the Constitution, and the writings of the Founding Fathers.

2. Educate our children. Give them hope. Set a positive example for them by our participation in our community, schools, and churches. Teach them that the way the world is today is not desirable for our happiness and that we can be a positive influence for good. Help them understand how they can distinguish between what they see and hear from their friends, the media, the government, and all that they do in life, and what is of real value and importance both to them and their children.

3. Work with the teachers' unions and show their leaders the damage that has been done by allowing freedom to be dropped from the curriculum in American public schools. Hundreds of thousands of American public school teachers do not agree with the policies of the NEA or the Department of Education—you probably know some who do not. Hundreds of thousands more teachers can see the results of decades of effort to replace rigorous academic standards with teachings on situation ethics, gender choice, condom use, and tolerance, all of which have contributed to today's extremely high dropout rates and the functional illiteracy of many who do survive and graduate.

4. Work with our local school districts to help them find ways to get around the Department of Education and NEA agendas - without losing essential Federal support - so that they may re-establish high academic standards and the teaching of principles like the duties and responsibilities of citizenship, the importance of moral conduct and integrity to the functioning of society, and more.

5. Create a non-profit charitable foundation whose sole purpose is to work with every PTA, college and university in the United States and help them establish courses on the Constitution. Some of these classes may eventually be taught by volunteers, which can reduce the costs to the school.

Those who are involved in this movement need to be confident in their knowledge and understanding. They need to be well grounded in the Constitution and the writings of the Founding Fathers. Only then can they be effective teachers and leaders, for they know what they know. We are not preaching the Gospel; if we were, we would be visited with more contention than we would wish. Instead, we "preach" freedom. In these days, helping others to become "converted" may be just as difficult for the one as it is for the other.

## Political Activism

We must be organized. We must have a national organization that solicits the input of its chapters and members and decides which issues must be addressed in the coming timeframes. The national organization must decide how to approach each issue, where the battles must be fought, and how we can win. Once those decisions have been made, the support of each member and chapter should be solicited and plans drawn up that will involve each of us.

Political activism is not necessarily a focus of a political party. I believe that the Constitution Party should partner in political activism with conservative organizations like the Tea Party Patriots, the Campaign for Liberty, and others. There should be a great deal of benefit and synergy to pooling our efforts and working toward common goals. It will also help the Constitution Party choose the battles that it will fight and make it more effective in the ones it chooses.

In recent years political activism has become less and less effective for conservative groups and more and more effective for liberal and special interest groups. It's almost hard to believe that just a few short years ago "political correctness" was lampooned in the media because it was advocated by a few people on the fringe of society. Those few have now become a very vocal and very large minority, and political correctness is the order of the day. Our rights of free speech as guaranteed in the First Amendment have been replaced by controlled speech. Politicians have seized on this and understood that they must pander to the groups promoting political correctness if they are to be elected and reelected.

We are now at the point where conservatives can safely be ignored by those on the left, for reasons we have explained previously. We should spend less time trying to get our elected officials and judges to change their minds, and more time trying to get the American people to recognize what is being done to them. Perhaps if your congressmen started receiving a half-million e-mails instead of the five or ten thousand he is currently receiving on an issue, he might be a little bit more inclined to listen.

Those additional e-mails will come from people who don't know what to do right now. Once they have made a commitment to support and defend the Constitution and begin receiving solid education on that document, they will add their voices to those calling for small government and individual sovereignty.

## A Recall Movement

I have an idea for political activism that is seldom if ever practiced and might be highly effective today. The Senate's power to impeach is exercised very seldom. Maybe we cannot expect the Senate to impeach one of its members (or the president or members of the House) on their failure to uphold their oath of office, for almost all senators frequently violate their oath. The Senate is a very powerful club and protects its own—or, at least, it protects those who "go along."

Instead, perhaps one particular Senator or Congressman should be singled out for especially egregious violations of his or her oath of office to support and defend the Constitution of the United States, and be subjected to a recall process. It would enable us to focus our resources on one relatively small geographic area and one small segment of the population, rather than trying to accomplish something that requires a majority of

Congress. Win or lose, such an event—if properly prosecuted—would send shivers through the halls of Congress, and issue a wake-up call to our elected officials much more powerful than the "pink slips" that were recently sent by angry voters.

The problem is that the Constitution does not provide a means whereby the people of the United States can issue a recall. With the passage of the Seventeenth Amendment (direct election of senators) even the state legislatures no longer have the power to recall a senator they sent to Washington. Our campaign would be conducted in the media and in public.

Should this representative or senator actually be recalled and replaced, there would be a great scramble on the part of our elected officials to get a hold of a copy of the Constitution and study it, perhaps for the first time in their lives. If they knew that they could be thrown out of office for violating their oath, they would think twice about voting in favor of socialist programs like national health care.

There would be another particular benefit to this as well. Elected judges would realize that they too are vulnerable, for they can be recalled the same as senators or congressmen. If they were to begin to fear for their tenure, their decisions might more closely reflect the Constitution and the intent of the Founding Fathers. When their decisions are reviewed by higher courts, do you think that an appellate court or the Supreme Court would be likely to reverse a decision that was clearly based upon the Constitution?

We must engage in political activism. We ought to make sure that whatever we do regarding political activism is as effective as possible, and that it promotes the purposes of our movement. It should also have quantifiable results, whether those results include getting a bill repealed, having a bill fail in Congress, or just in creating public awareness in the minds of the electorate. Each act of political activism should be carefully planned based upon the quantifiable results obtained in all previous actions. We should get better at what we do, and we will as we discover the real strengths and weaknesses of our elected officials.

# Lobbying

Finally, we have to engage in lobbying. In some ways this puts us on the defensive, for most of us don't like lobbyists, and we don't like what they do. Lobbyists generally represent groups with lots of money or particular self-interests or both, and seek to obtain something from elected officials that the majority would not approve.

Our lobbying will not involve coercion, bribery, arm-twisting, blackmail, or making large campaign contributions. It will also not involve distorting the truth or seeking benefits on behalf of a small segment of the population. Our lobbying will, if successful, benefit all Americans living and yet to be born. Tyler Cowen said this:

> "For all the anecdotal evidence, it's hard to show statistically that money has a large and systematic influence on political outcomes. That is partly because politicians cannot stray too far from public opinion. (In part, is also because interest groups get their way on many issues by supplying an understaffed Congress with ideas and intellectual resources, not by running ads or make innovations.)"[9]

Our lobbying will be focused upon building good working relationships with our elected officials and judges, and proving to them that we will always support the principles of the Constitution and the ideals of the Founding Fathers. Sooner or later our elected officials will begin to realize how very important what we say really is, and we will gain their respect. When we have earned that respect and trust we will begin to be able to influence legislation far beyond the abilities of those who have been elected as Constitution Party candidates. It will not happen overnight, but it will happen if we are consistent and honest.

As for the media, no trend continues forever. As we labor to educate ourselves and our fellow Americans about the Constitution, we will begin the long and slow process of sweeping away all the misinformation, the deliberate falsehoods, the polarization, the name-calling, and all the other negative practices of the media today. Our opinions will become valuable in the eyes of at least some in the media, and if they wish for us to express those ideas they will have to provide us with a proper opportunity to do so. If we do not respond in kind, those who have made fortunes for themselves by heaping abuse upon us and all those who hold to high standards will begin to look foolish and will lose their audiences. Again, this will take time, and we need to be consistent and exercise the highest levels of integrity in all that we do. This covers a lot of ground. Before we go into specifics, let's consider how we need to portray ourselves.

## CHAPTER EIGHTEEN

# How Do We Portray Ourselves? An Essay

In every public expression made by members of this organization, we must occupy the moral high ground and hold it. In addition, we must be kind, patient, persuasive, well informed—and long-suffering. We dare not stoop to the level of our opponents, for when we do we lose.

"I may not agree with what you say, but I will defend to the death your right to say it." I think that homily may have gotten lost. We are supposed to be "the good guys"; we are the people who want to bring respect, decency, civility, integrity, and morality back to the national debate. Of course there will always be those who are ignorant, misinformed, downright stupid, holding fast to uninformed opinions, and just plain haters of everything that is good—but if they are American citizens they have the right to say what they wish.

How much better might it be if someone were to sit down one-on-one with those individuals who oppose us, show them our position paper and the Constitution we love and defend, and see if they won't change their minds. People do change their minds, you know. There are many who are not so conditioned in their responses that they can no longer distinguish black from white. If they won't change, and if they persist in opposing the principles of freedom, they make themselves the type of people who will accomplish little of value in this life and who will be forgotten in death. We don't have to concern ourselves with them, but we may need to repair the damage they do.

How can we fight politically correct speech if we too wish to restrict speech of any type? How can we legally suppress dissent without becoming autocrats? Or, as I said during the Bush administration, when we engage in torture (speaking of Guantanamo Bay and Iraq), are we any better than the enemy?

We need to hold to the standards of the Founding Fathers we revere. Or maybe we need to be good Christians and turn the other cheek.

For decades the Left has made conservatives look like fools because they took a "holier than thou" air and mocked us. They made the world believe that they had superior minds and superior ideas. We let them do so because we were disorganized. We had never conceived of having to defend the foundational principles of morality and decency on which our lives were based. We allowed pornography because they said it was "free speech." We allowed abortion because they said it was "a choice." We allowed gay marriage because they said we were denying them their rights. *They* have been applying all the labels. *They* have controlled the dialogue. *They* have made the accusations of racism, bigotry, war-mongers, empire builders, and every other epithet—all to put us at a disadvantage and elevate themselves to the [immoral] high ground.

They have had their day in the sun. Their programs and ideas are as bankrupt as the countries they took over. Liberalism has so dominated the media, public education, the halls of Congress, the courts, and the public dialogue that we have not yet begun to turn the corner and reveal the true face of socialism. That day will come, but not as a result of us soiling ourselves with the same mud they have been throwing.

If we do not choose the battleground but let them choose it instead, we will continue to lose. If we descend to their level of vulgarity, dishonesty, immorality, and empty promises, we are no better than them.

I believe we *must* set the example of truth, fair play, decency, and civility. I could not participate in tactics like those used by the Left. Remember, their methods have infected Democrats and Republicans alike. Even the Libertarians seem to have been seduced into a corruption of their basic beliefs regarding victimless crimes, which has led to tacit approval of the horrors of abortion and the destructive effects of immorality.

Personally, I will not lie, cheat, nor steal to defend the Constitution. I will not defame nor attempt to defame another because his beliefs (or his public outbursts) are meant to discredit me. I will speak the truth as I understand it and teach others a love of liberty. I will teach them the principles Americans seem to have lost—of the right to liberty and property, of the right to work hard to obtain a living without a massive bureaucracy critiquing their every move. I will teach that all men are equal under the law, that they may exercise freedom of conscience, and that they will be held responsible for their actions.

If we speak with the voice of reason, of kindness, and of charity, we will the more effectively silence those who rail on us. Their noise will be seen as foolishness, and their preaching will ring as hollow as it really is.

I can't feel more strongly about this. I can think of two incidents during his mortal ministry when Jesus exercised righteous indignation, and in both instances he cleansed the Temple—literally His Father's house. On no occasion did he ever lift his hand to curse a human being—that condemnation was reserved for a fig tree. Rather, he taught that we should love our enemies, bless those who curse us, and pray for them who despitefully use and persecute us. He then told us why that was so important (Matthew 5:45–47). If we act as our detractors do, *ours is the greater sin.* Why? Because we know better. Do we really want to be the Pharisees?

We will catch more flies with honey than with vinegar. We want to recruit into our ranks those who can carry in their hearts the spark of freedom that motivated our Founding Fathers. If you read the commentaries of those assembled in the Constitutional Convention you will be amazed. Many of them expressed astonishment at how men of strong opinions set aside their beliefs and ideas in favor of something bigger and more important than themselves. The miracle of the Constitution is that a group of men were able to establish a wonderful Constitution *almost in spite of themselves.*

The people who got us into this mess are not the ones who will get us out. We do not need those who are bound to a defunct and rotting political philosophy, nor those who must be bribed into every action they take. We need to educate the people of these United States about the true meaning of freedom so that they may choose for themselves whether they truly want—and deserve—that government of the people, by the people, and for the people we are trying to help them create. We will drive them away, and they will refuse to listen if our voices are as strident and critical as those who stand against us.

## Americans need to know:

The Constitution is the most important legal document ever produced by any group of individuals because it limits the power of central government and guarantees certain freedoms to the citizens of the nation it created.

The Constitution is as viable today as it was in 1787. Its usefulness as the foundation of our republic is unchanged.

Americans have allowed themselves to be seduced by the appeal of "getting something for nothing" from their government.

The federal government today does not honor, support, or sustain the Constitution.

Significant change is required if we are to restore the United States to its constitutional foundation.

That change will not be without pain or difficulty, because many who have received benefits "from the public trough" will see those benefits cease.

Those who love freedom and the Constitution are not radicals nor anarchists. Likewise, they are not socialists. They are people like you and me who love this country and want to see it fulfill its potential as a free land, offering opportunity to all who are willing to work hard and live moral, decent lives.

The American people have nothing to fear from the Tea Party Patriots or the Constitution Party. What we strive to achieve is what people throughout history have longed for.

Restoring the Constitution to its rightful place in our government will help Americans become far more compassionate and charitable. It will help us to put in their place those who would perform "social engineering" and impose "shock and awe" in an effort to make us forget the blessings of freedom.

The Constitution as originally framed and amended through the years will need some modifications to brought back into line with the intention of the Founding Fathers in light of today's environment. Some of the amendments need to be strengthened and others repealed. Certain aspects of government and of society need to be held in check to avoid a tyranny of the minority. These changes include prohibiting the judiciary from "legislating from the bench" and dictating our moral code; preventing presidents from drafting Executive Orders that are given the force of law; fixing the system of campaign contributions, which is so prone to abuse; reducing and eliminating hundreds of thousands of jobs in the federal bureaucracy that were created through unconstitutional legislation; and more. The activities of lobbying groups must be fully disclosed. No agency or branch of government must ever be permitted to lobby another.

These changes cannot be dictated from above, for no one in a position of power ever wants to change the status quo unless it will expand his or her authority and power. They must come through the legal process of public debate, seeking of consensus, and action by legislators as informed by their constituents. Unfortunately, with the current low level of understanding of Constitutional principles among the American people in our day and the strident voice of those who stand in opposition to those principles, we are not now prepared to engage in such a debate. If we did, the principles of freedom would lose.

"The creed of our democracy is that liberty is acquired and kept by men and women who are strong and self-reliant, and possessed of such wisdom as God gives mankind—men and women who are just, and understanding, and generous to others—men and women who are capable of disciplining themselves. For they are the rulers and they must rule themselves."
—*Franklin D. Roosevelt*, 10/28/44

★ CHAPTER NINETEEN ★

# What Must be Done *Now* to Restore America to its Constitutional Foundation

M y "vision" of this project involves these elements:

1. Member recruitment
2. Member education and training
3. Fund-raising
4. Making the knowledge of the Constitution available to the American people
5. Party leader recruitment and training
6. Candidate recruitment and training
7. Political activism
8. Expansion across the country
9. Local and national media campaign
10. Lobbying
11. Ballot access
12. Promoting Constitution Party candidates

Each of those things is part of the whole, and little can be accomplished if any one of them fails. A group like the Tea Party Patriots can do some but not all of the things on this list. *Only* a political party can do everything on the list. Let's look at each of them in more detail.

Note: I use the term "committee" rather loosely in this section. The term committee in this context refers to the local (usually a county or precinct) group of Constitution Party members organized to accomplish all the items above in their local area. These committees may also be called chapters or precincts; the words are interchangeable.

# 1. Member Recruitment

## *Key Points:*

- Members recruit new members from among their friends, family, neighbors, fellow church members, and business associates.

- Members are trained in recruiting techniques at each chapter meeting.

- Most of the time members invite, but the actual recruiting is performed at the committee meeting by volunteer "recruiters".

- New members complete a Talents and Abilities Survey to help determine how they might most effectively serve in the organization.

- Those with specific talents or interests will be groomed and trained either for leadership within the party or to run for and serve in elective office.

I remember an experience in Philadelphia many years ago. I was with a group of people, all of them American citizens, and a man dressed up as Benjamin Franklin was addressing us. At one point our national anthem began to play, and my wife and I were the only people in the room who stood up. The man playing the part of Benjamin Franklin, who had been standing as he addressed us, had to ask the rest of the group to please rise for the national anthem.

These were Americans like you and me who were interested in American history and who wanted to know more about it. These families were raising their children to be good citizens. They chose to attend that presentation in part because they love this country, and yet they failed to either recognize or acknowledge our national anthem. If they had been at a baseball game, undoubtedly all of them would have stood immediately—though perhaps only because the announcer asked everyone to stand for the playing of the national anthem.

Patriotism seems "so last century" these days. We often act as if we are ashamed of our country, and perhaps there are good reasons for feeling that way. We should be ashamed that America projects military might into more than 125 countries around the world, for we have no business being in those countries "protecting American interests." America should be the world's business partner, and pay in full for what we receive from outside our borders. If we have a sound currency, all the world will sell to us. We have no right to attempt to disrupt the government of any country to suit our purposes, nor to use "the big stick" to force compliance with our doctrines whether they are morally and ethically defensible or not.

We should be ashamed that one of America's primary exports to the world is not freedom but Hollywood with all its filth and immorality. We should be particularly ashamed that America has undermined its own moral foundation by legalizing abortion, sexual promiscuity, sexual perversion, and the right of the state to step in and break up families it deems dysfunctional. Worse, we are trying diligently to force those evils upon the rest of the world, as witness America's efforts at the United Nations regarding the "rights" of children and all women's rights to freely available abortion. This is far from the Founder's vision of what America should represent to the world.

In many ways the image America portrays to its citizens and to outsiders is reprehensible. We must not focus on the way things are today, however; our task is to make the future better. If we can awaken in the American people the decency most of them possess, and help them to stand up to judges who legislate morality from the bench and a Congress that seizes power through enslaving its constituents, we may once again have an America we can be proud of. We have no reason to be proud of being a bully, or advancing an empty and immoral philosophy as we are and do today.

It may take a long time for the pendulum to reverse and move back toward the Constitution, but if Americans can be reminded of their potential as individuals and as citizens, we can make great strides. Many Americans know that much is wrong in America today, but they are unaware of the magnitude of the problem and are not organized to create effective change. Americans are encouraged by their government to apply for as many benefits as possible, for this is the way in which government enslaves us.

The appeal of the welfare state is ever with us. We hear it every day of our lives. We need to hear the voice of freedom proclaimed across the land; we need to be called into action to save our Republic from those who would destroy it. The cry of Freedom needs to be heard in every home, school, factory, church, shop, and office, and a banner raised to which men and women of conscience may rally. Our government demands little of us today, and we respond by becoming smaller and smaller people with reduced hopes and expectations. By raising the flag of freedom we will ask Americans to take on a great cause that will require their best efforts. The only way they will respond favorably is if they can see that victory is possible. To encourage people to leave our spiritual and moral Babylon we must show them the city on the hill which is a light unto all nations.

Americans become more patriotic when our nation is threatened. We become more civic- minded when our immediate family is threatened by things that are going on in our local community. Getting involved is usually inconvenient and takes us away from the things we would rather be doing, and for this reason Americans are considered to be great "joiners" but relatively poor active participants.

Because of this attitude—and it is by no means unique to Americans—we tend to "let things slide" when we don't feel that our current situation is threatened. Our enemies—both internal and external—have discovered that tendency and capitalized on it. For decades Americans have been taught little in the public schools about the Constitution and the wisdom of the founding fathers. Instead, we have been fed a steady stream of information about what is wrong with our Constitution, with capitalism, with free enterprise, and so on. Bad legislation is written into law because there is a little something in there for every congressman or senator whose vote is required for passage. That "little something" must be money or a project that the legislator can bring back to the folks at home, and show them that he's doing his job by grabbing a piece of the federal pie.

At the same time we have been fed all sorts of notions about rights, and how we have rights far above and beyond those guaranteed to us by the Constitution. Most Americans are comfortable with these new rights as long as they don't interfere with our lifestyle. Just like the frogs in a frying pan full of water, we tend not to "jump out" as the water is heated because the rise in temperature is gradual. The American people should have jumped out of this "frying pan" years ago.

Because we have been absolutely inundated with liberal and socialistic ideas, our public dialogue and even our way of thinking have been radically altered. Not too many years ago most Americans refused to take a handout from anyone; they were proud people and would do whatever it took to get through a crisis. They were more honest, more faithful, and more knowledgeable regarding the blessings of freedom. Today we have allowed ourselves to become convinced that "the world owes us a living," and we happily accept handouts from our government. Little do we realize what a canker to the soul these handouts really are.

Many of us have convinced ourselves that we don't really receive any benefits from the government; all we do is pay our taxes and hope to get a small refund each year. Government today intrudes into every aspect of our lives, and all of us are feeding at the public trough in one way or another.

I believe the only way to change this is to educate the American people about their Constitution and the wisdom of the founding fathers. We don't all need to become Constitutional scholars, but we ought to be able to hold our own in defending the Constitution and recognizing when the acts of any branch of government violate it. Big government becomes bigger when the people allow it to do so. Each new intrusion into our lives is met with a shrug; after all, the government is only looking out for our best interests—or is it?

How do we go about this educational process? We can't go to the public schools, for many of them are dominated by the liberal teachers' unions. We can't go to the public or the private universities, for most of them are hotbeds of liberalism and radical thought.

We need to go to the people directly. We need to find those who are dissatisfied with our government and ask them to join our movement. It is not enough to ask people to sign a petition or even to make a contribution to a political candidate or a political action committee. Doing something like that may give the individual a brief feeling of having done something worthwhile, but it doesn't last, and it doesn't make that person any better. It's more like the brief euphoria that certain illegal drugs can produce; it doesn't change anything except to impoverish the user and make him even more dependent.

We need to hold regular meetings of this Constitution Party, and in those regular meetings introduce and welcome newcomers. Every member of the group should be encouraged to bring someone else to the next meeting.

Each member should sign a written pledge that details the purposes of the organization. By signing that pledge and by taking an oath, that individual agrees to become more actively involved in the political process. We need to ask three things of him or her: time, talents, and resources.

For example, each member should be asked to contribute $100 per year to the organization, and perhaps $150 for a married couple and $200 for an entire family. If necessary, these contributions can be made using automatic bank drafts, or the organization should accept credit cards.

Each member should commit a minimum of one hour per week to the cause (not counting their personal study time). During that time the member will learn about the Constitution and the issues of the day, learn how to recruit people into the organization, invite his friends, neighbors, and business associates to the organization's regular meetings, attend the regular meetings, and be involved in political activism. One hour per week is inadequate to accomplish all this, but it is a start.

Each member would complete a *Talents and Abilities Survey* describing his experience, his hobbies, his education, and the things he likes to do as well as the things he does well. There is a great need for trained leadership in the organization, and a great need for dedicated and reliable candidates for political office.

There are many ways in which people may be recruited. Each member ought to be taught how to approach his neighbor, ask to be invited into the neighbor's home, and sit down with them and share his or her feelings about the Constitution and what we are trying to accomplish. That will be the most effective way of finding those who love freedom and who will be willing to defend it—once they know there is a national organization that has that as its primary purpose.

Recruitment can also take place when our friends and neighbors are invited to participate with us in Tea Parties and other political rallies, petition drives, and educational sessions.

Some people will be reluctant to join the organization until they are convinced that we are supporting the principles of freedom rather than a particular party or candidate.

Statistically, if every member simply brought someone else with them to the next meeting, and if that person joined the organization, membership would double at each meeting. That will not happen, of course, and even if it did we would not have trained leadership in place to accommodate it. We must grow at a rapid but appropriate pace so that we may meet the needs of all our members.

## 2. Member Education and Training

### Key Points:

- Each member is given a "recommended reading" list with a schedule. The schedule coincides with the educational sessions held during committee meetings. In this way members of each committee or chapter are reading the same things at the same time, and can discuss what we have read in our classes.

- Each member completes the basic constitution course before progressing to the regular educational program.

- Both educational "tracks" run simultaneously and continuously.

Education is the key to everything the Party does. Americans must learn about the Constitution and why it is so vital to our freedom and our happiness. If we are to restore America to the Constitution, we must not only understand the issues and what our leaders are doing wrong; we must know what they should be doing instead and help them see the Constitutional path. Often our leaders give in to pressure because they have no viable alternatives.

Two classes should be held at each [monthly] meeting. One is a basic class on the Constitution for all new members and guests. It might last as long as twenty-four lessons and be taught in rotation—which implies that monthly meetings will not be enough. There must be homework, of course, for thirty minutes of class time is quite inadequate to obtain a good understanding of just about anything.

The other course will focus on current issues and Constitutional solutions. All who have completed the Basic course will attend this class at each meeting. Classes will be taught by members on a rotating basis so that all have an opportunity to prepare a lesson and teach it. This will build confidence and help members gain valuable experience in public speaking.

Member training will be conducted by Committee leaders specifically trained and qualified to do so. Training will include many behavioral topics such as inviting friends and neighbors to meetings, conducting interviews, engaging in political activism, letter writing, public speaking, recruitment, teaching, leadership, and running a political campaign.

# 3. Fundraising

## Key Points:

- Members arrange to make their annual $100 contribution either immediately upon taking the Pledge or in installments, as appropriate. Additional contributions are always welcome and will be solicited through various channels.

- Contributions are allocated according to a predetermined formula between the local committee and the state and national organizations.

- Members may always know how their contributions are being utilized.

Fundraising is often frowned upon in organizations because the leaders are concerned it will drive away the members. That might be true in an organization that is not working on something worthwhile and understandable, but it is not the case with us. We have the example before us of the Founding Fathers, who were willing to sacrifice their lives, their fortunes, and their sacred honor in the defense of freedom. In a very real sense we ask that of our members, but we give them an opportunity to grow in the movement and strengthen their commitment as they continue to participate. We would hope that through their association with the organization they will gain a desire to participate more fully in this vital effort. Some can contribute time and talents, others money, and some may be placed in a position to be of influence in critical moments.

Every member will know where his contributions go. There must always be full disclosure, not only to meet the requirements of the law, but to help members understand what their contributions are helping to accomplish.

One hundred dollars a year isn't much, but for the kind of people we want to recruit it may be more than they contribute during the course of a year to anything except their church. Special contributions may be solicited from time to time, but the focus of our meeting should never be fundraising. For their one hundred dollars, each member should be given a membership card, which will serve as a reminder of the commitment they made.

I do not believe that we should ever attempt to raise funds outside of our membership. Rather, I believe that we should try to increase our membership rapidly and utilize the volunteers wherever possible in leadership positions in order to minimize the organization's expenses. We must be an organization of volunteers.

# 4. Making the knowledge of the Constitution available to the American people

---

*Key Points:*

- Each local Committee of the Constitution Party has as part of its responsibility the task of working with local school districts, colleges and universities to ensure that the Constitution is regularly and properly taught in each of those institutions.

- The Constitution Party may form a separate foundation to produce and distribute appropriate materials for teaching the Constitution at all levels, or it may work with existing organizations such as the National Center for Constitutional Studies (NCCS).

- This effort may or may not be considered part of our recruiting work, though eventually many new Party recruits will come from the ranks of those who have learned about the Constitution through our efforts.

---

This is the heart of the matter. This is where we will have our greatest success as we make it possible for Americans to understand and revere their Constitution once again. We must portray the Constitution as the law of the land and always demonstrate very clearly why it is superior to any other political document in the way it protects our freedoms and grants us opportunities to improve our situation to the best of our ability.

Coupled with a greatly expanded effort to teach people about the Constitution will be the effort to educate people about the fallacies and pernicious doctrines of the Universal Declaration of Human Rights. We cannot merely warn people that the shift away from the Constitution will lead to slavery and destruction; we must show them exactly how it has happened in the past and how and why it will happen here if we proceed on our present course. It will be easy to present the Constitution to many of those who pay taxes in the United States, but it will be a much more difficult "sell" to the rest of the American people who have become accustomed to being taken care of by government. It will take a great deal of study and thought to create a curriculum that will convince such people to move away from the welfare state.

# 5. Party Leader recruitment and training

## *Key Points:*

- In order for the Party to grow we need thousands of active local committees whose leaders will devote several hours per week to the Party.

- Party leader candidates will be interviewed and recruited by current local Party leaders.

- Each local committee will have 17 officers, of which 11 will comprise the local Executive Council.

- The 11 local committee officers who comprise the Executive Council are:

> Committee Head
> Assistant Committee Head
> Treasurer
> Committee Secretary
> Committee Historian
> Activities Coordinator
> Education Coordinator
> Committee Website Editor
> Trainer
> Teacher, Continuing Education Class
> Ballot Access Specialist

- The other six local committee officers are:

  Teacher, Basic Class
  Alternate Teacher
  Alternate Trainer
  Recruiters (2)
  Website Developer

- Local Committees should have between 40 and 150 members. When a local Committee has more than 150 members, it should be divided.

In this volunteer organization all of us should be utilized as effectively as possible. That's why all new members complete the *Talents and Abilities Survey*—so that the leaders of each local committee know something about the capabilities and experience of each member. Leadership positions should be rotated so that many people have the opportunity to serve as leaders and teachers. The local committee leader, for example, might serve for a minimum of twelve months, whereas a teacher might serve for six months, or two or three teachers might teach the same class for a year or two in rotation.

It is the duty of the committee leader to prepare the members of his group to serve in the numerous assignments available to them. The committee leader works regularly with his Executive Committee to ensure that all those who are serving in leadership and teaching positions in the committee are properly trained and motivated and are being as effective as possible in their respective positions. The Executive Committee also helps to decide what changes will be made.

At each monthly meeting all attendees will participate in the Training portion of the meeting, except for those who are new members and guests who have not yet completed the basic Constitution class. This training should be beneficial to every aspect of our lives, not just our service to the Constitution Party.

Is also important that teachers be rotated frequently so that everyone has a chance to teach. The teacher always learns more than the student, and in addition to gaining knowledge about the subject matter the teacher gains experience in assembling materials, creating a syllabus, conducting the class, and obtaining feedback from class members. All of these are valuable skills that can assist us with our families, in our careers, and in every other aspect of our lives. Since so few of us really understand the Constitution and the writings of the Founding Fathers well enough to freely discuss and defend them, teaching about them gives us first-hand experience with these wonderful concepts and ideas. Simply pondering them increases our understanding of, and appreciation for, the Founding Fathers.

Service as a leader in the Party is a privilege and an opportunity for personal growth. Because this is a volunteer organization, all of us serve because we want to. We should look upon serving in Party leadership as an opportunity to grow and to gain skills and experience that will help us in promoting and defending the Constitution. It will also help us in other aspects of our lives, for we will be working with people who have their own ideas, motivations, and agendas. The challenge of leadership is to motivate and inspire people to work together in a common cause.

We should never consider that there is one ideal person for each leadership position, or that any person will serve in one position indefinitely. Instead, leadership should rotate frequently, perhaps annually, to give all of our members the opportunity to serve in a leadership capacity.

All party members should be trained to serve as Party officers. Membership in the Constitution Party does not mean that we will serve in Party leadership, but each of us should expect to do so and prepare for it. If we are to be effective we must fill all of the fifteen to twenty leadership positions in each county or regional committee. Each person must be trained in the specifics of his or her assignment, and his progress monitored by the Committee leader. As in any organization, as people gain experience serving in Party leadership they will become better at what they do and qualify themselves to serve in other positions.

It will be important to avoid the old syndrome of "the same ten people" who do everything. Each member will have an assignment, whether he or she is a Party leader or not. Assignments may include letter writing, press releases, media events, political activism, lobbying, research, and more. County committees will focus primarily on local issues; however, once a strong national Party leadership is in place we will also become involved in state and federal issues. Members need to be trained to work in the various levels of the Party organization and to interface with other committees and share ideas. Our classes should not be lectures; instead, they should utilize appropriate techniques to promote active participation by class members and optimize the learning experience.

Party leadership positions are filled by common consent. When a committee is newly organized and spun off from an existing committee, each member of the new committee will vote to sustain the slate of officers compiled by the executive committee of the existing committee.

## 6. Candidate recruitment and training

### Key Points:

- Those who qualify to run for public office are identified through an interview with the Committee leader. Some candidates will be selected by the local Executive Committee; others will come to the Party for support.

- State and National candidates for office will be selected at the appropriate levels within the Party. All must "pass muster" and hold fast to the principles of the Constitution.

Thousands of elections are held each cycle in which one candidate runs unopposed. This should not be the case wherever the Constitution Party is organized and viable. What better way to create public awareness of our existence than to obtain ballot access for candidates who are firmly grounded in the Constitution, and who love and appreciate it?

Most of those elections with unopposed candidates are local elections, but because of gerrymandering there are many congressional districts where the congressman runs unopposed, particularly in cases where that congressman is the chairman of a powerful committee or is a Party leader.

Part of our job as members of the Constitution Party is to identify, recruit, and train those who will run for public office at all levels. We really shouldn't be voting for someone running for president of the United States who was unknown two years earlier. The Founding Fathers did not envision "career politicians" as we have today, but they did envision a nation of people who knew and understood their Constitution and who worked together to put good, God-fearing men and women into public office. What better place to produce those candidates than the Constitution Party?

One of the most wonderful things about the Constitution Party is that it is basically a grassroots organization, which means that we can make significant inroads at the local level through the workings of our local and county committees. If we could place hundreds of Constitution Party members into local elective office, the entire country would come to know that the Constitution party exists. That would prompt many hundreds of thousands of Americans to look into the Constitution Party and discover what we have to offer. Participation in and winning local elections will be a springboard to state and national office, and a much easier path than running national candidates who receive little or no financial or media support from the Constitution Party.

# 7. Political activism

*Key Points:*

- All activism by the organization will promote a Constitutional alternative to the legislation currently being proposed or debated.

- We will always be for something rather than against everything.

- We will show the American people why the Constitution works and is viable in its original form. We will also point out where the Founding Fathers did not succeed in establishing sufficient checks upon the federal government.

Many Americans seem to have a natural feel for political activism. They enjoy shaking hands with their fellow citizens in local events, inviting people to sign petitions, and in promoting letter writing campaigns, boycotts, and demonstrations. We don't often think of political parties as being heavily involved in political activism, in part because both the Democratic and Republican Party conduct such activities through affiliate organizations. However, political activism is something a political party can and should do.

One of the things that political activism can accomplish for us is to create public awareness of the existence of the Constitution Party. The Republicans and Democrats don't need to advertise that they exist, but we do. We need to promote ourselves and our platform and create a genuine impression of integrity and respectability if we have any hope of success in this work.

Our political activism is one of the ways in which we promote Constitutional alternatives to the actions of government. We won't be there just to protest something; we will be there to show the American people and our elected and appointed officials the *right* way to do things.

# 8. Expansion across the country

---

### Key Points:

- Local Committees will be added only when trained and qualified leaders are available.

- Members will have a say in when the time is right for a committee to divide.

- Members should invite friends who live far away to meetings of the closest committee.

---

The Party must achieve rapid growth if we are to have any hope of restoring America to its Constitutional foundation. However, growth must not proceed in the absence of trained and qualified local committee leaders. Since the Constitution Party as a political party has the legal right to organize, recruit members, promote candidates, obtain ballot access, and solicit and collect contributions and dues, we need to make sure that we are well organized everywhere the Party is found.

Each member of the Party is too precious to risk losing to differences of opinion, lack of leadership, failure to coordinate, or anything else that will drive people away. Besides, we are and must always remember that we are a volunteer organization, and that each of us allocates our own valuable time and resources to this great cause because we want to.

Though the bulk of the work of recruitment is handled at the grassroots level, as the organization grows and gains a presence in each state and at the federal level we will begin to take steps that will recruit people who have not yet come into contact with our grassroots efforts. The technology available today is such that we can have isolated, unorganized individuals and groups who belong to the Constitution party who are waiting for a Party committee to be organized in their area.

This is one of the areas where "critical mass" will be very significant. When the Party reaches a certain level of activity it will have gained sufficient credibility and recognition to begin to attract individuals and groups.

## 9. Local and national media campaigns

### Key Points:

- The Party will take advantage of all the free publicity it can get, being careful to avoid debates and adverse situations where the playing field cannot be made level.

- The national organization will issue regular press releases regarding current issues. Leaders at all levels may engage the press to advance public awareness.

The Constitution Party must keep the Constitution before the people of the United States as much as possible. I would like to see a Constitution Channel available 24/7 on its own cable network, providing high-quality commentary on the issues of the day, classes on the Constitution, presentations from various experts on topics like state sovereignty, judicial activism, national health care, global warming, and much more.

It will always be appropriate to have Constitution Party videos available on YouTube and elsewhere showcasing the Constitution and the way Americans ought to feel about it. Well-executed materials will build our credibility and our reputation.

# 10. Lobbying

## Key Points:

- Lobbying is a fact of life. Though expensive, it must be pursued by the Party at all appropriate levels of government.

- The primary emphasis of our lobbying effort will be to support Constitutional principles, and to provide ways for elected officials to sustain them.

Today, lobbying is the way things get done in Washington. That must be changed, because much of government centers around influence peddling and significant pressure on our elected officials from special interest groups, all of them seeking preferential treatment. Just about every industry in the country has its own lobbying organization. Many express their wishes by making campaign contributions, and those who are elected because of those contributions are beholden to them.

This organization will need to lobby as well, and I believe much of our effort will be toward convincing our elected officials of the constitutionality (or lack thereof) of the legislation they are currently considering. If we can just "hold their feet to the fire" and make them realize that there are people in the United States who will hold them accountable for the observance of their oath of office, we should be able to effect some changes.

Since we are concerned with national issues, I believe it would be appropriate for a means to be devised whereby the ideas and opinions of Party members might be solicited. In this way leaders of the organization can be guided in their lobbying efforts, and devote appropriate time and resources to important issues. If we are trying to restore a truly representative government, our organization ought to function in a similar manner.

Lobbying is a very expensive activity, but it does get results when it is done properly. The question the Party must answer is whether lobbying within the existing system will be as beneficial as the use of the same resources elsewhere to recruit and educate the American people. For the foreseeable future it seems obvious that the Party's limited resources must be devoted primarily to building its base and creating a constituency for the Constitution.

What would the Party lobby for? Where appropriate, we should always represent the Constitution and present without bias the ideas put forth by the Founding Fathers on each subject. When we are dealing with issues that are "extra-Constitutional," our emphasis would be to encourage our government to pursue that course most consistent with the ideals of freedom.

In other words, we would lobby to protect natural rights and all that is found in the Bill of Rights. We might also take every possible step to reduce America's involvement with foreign nations, rather than being "nation builders." On social issues and human rights, we need to help our leaders understand their oath of office in their obligation to support natural rights and the sovereignty of the United States.

# 11. Ballot Access

## Key Points:

- Each local Committee will have a Ballot Access Specialist who will work to obtain ballot access for all races in which the Constitution Party will run candidates.

- The Ballot Access Specialist may have one or more assistants who will coordinate their efforts.

- Additional Ballot Access Specialists will be appointed as appropriate at the State and Federal levels.

Ballot access takes a great deal of time and effort, and it is a significant drain on Party resources. It is also extremely important, for it keeps the party viable and offers its members and others the opportunity to run for and serve in elective office as people who believe in and defend the Constitution. If anything, we must commit additional resources and manpower to ballot access, just as we must spend time training Party members and recruiting them and others to run for office with the support of the Constitution Party.

The effort to obtain ballot access in many political jurisdictions will also keep election officials aware of who we are and what we are trying to do. If we can make friends in such places and demonstrate that we have the interests of our country at heart, we can reduce the opposition of the Republicans and others, and eventually have an easier time of getting our candidates on the ballot.

If the Party would take my suggestion to heart and begin to specifically identify, recruit, train, and support Party members to run in elections where one candidate would otherwise be running unopposed, and if we helped each candidate to obtain his own ballot access, we would make a major leap forward. In most cases those running in these elections would have a significantly better chance of success, with the possible exception of "safe" districts which have been gerrymandered to specifically favor the party currently in power. Now that we have seen that there can be a backlash powerful enough to give Ted Kennedy's seat to a Republican, this idea is looking better and better.

# 12. Promoting Constitution Party Candidates

---

## Key Points:

- Candidates for elective office will come from three main sources:
- Candidate switching from other parties,
- Candidates chosen by the Constitution party, and
- Candidates who choose to run on their own, and seek the support of the Constitution Party.
- The Constitution Party will support all those who run as CP candidates, as long as they uphold all the standards and the platform of the Party.
- Constitution Party members can and should assist in all campaign activities for CP candidates. This includes fundraising, staffing campaign headquarters, arranging for media exposure, participation in local events, and more.

---

Political candidates at all levels must do a tremendous amount of work if they want to win. The major parties provide them with funding and staff, and they also recruit volunteers to help out in their election campaigns. The Constitution Party does these things as well, though on a shoestring budget. We need to identify and effectively utilize the most inexpensive sources of publicity available. We need to closely couple the candidate with the message, for that will differentiate a Constitution Party candidate from anyone else.

There is a great deal of valuable experience to be gained in running a political campaign. It will be good to involve as many people as possible, for all will learn much, and some will someday be running for office themselves. I believe this is how the

American system was meant to work—that we would run for and win election to local offices and work our way up the ladder to state and then to national office, always keeping in mind that there is no such thing as a "career politician" in the United States. If we worked together and supported and sustained one another, we could produce a constant supply of qualified, honest people who would run for office under the banner of the Constitution Party who will do everything they can to support and defend the Constitution.

## How to Do It: Recruitment

There are many opportunities to recruit new members into the Constitution Party. Our members need to be trained in recognizing opportunities as well as in inviting those around them to attend a meeting.

Our political activism will be an important source of new recruits. As we participate in gun shows, Tea Parties, and meetings of other conservative organizations we can invite people to "see for themselves." This invitation should be extended when we think the person is interested in defending the Constitution and might be willing to work with us. We should never "step on the toes" of other organizations like the Campaign for Liberty; at the same time, they need to realize that we are trying to work together, and that the Constitution Party can do things that their organization simply cannot. Always remember that we are trying to become unified in our efforts to restore the Constitution, and that our current fragmented situation has made little or no progress.

The primary way people will be invited to one of our meetings is through the personal invitations of our members. Constitution Party members should accept the challenge to bring one new person to each meeting. That alone would be significant to create significant growth in Party membership, but it would tend to exclude those we know who are distant from us.

All of us know people who are interested in the cause of freedom but who live in other parts of the country. We should produce a standard invitation letter and brochure, which our members can mail to their friends, relatives, and associates who live in other areas. This letter and brochure would specifically reference the local Constitution Party organization in their area so that they may be invited to participate in a group that is already in operation.

For those who live in neighboring towns and adjacent counties, they should be invited to attend one meeting with the person who invites them. That person can attend his own meeting and bring his friend with him, or that person can invite their friends to attend a meeting in the area where the friend lives. If the friend lives in an area that does not yet have a Constitution Party group, the friend could become the first member of a group that is yet to be formed.

We need to recruit people in all walks of life and in all economic strata. As members we invite; we do not take it upon ourselves to pre-judge whether someone will or will not join the Party before we even extend the invitation.

When a Party member brings a friend or associate to one of our meetings for the first time, the member should remain with his friend or associate for the entire meeting, except perhaps when the guest is interviewed by a recruiter. This helps to make the guests feel much more comfortable in attending our meeting, and more likely to benefit from it.

We should build strong friendships with one another as members of the Constitution Party. We are good people who are trying to become better, and we are engaged in a great and important work. We should lead exemplary lives. We should be compassionate and caring, and we should help others to gain the skills necessary to be an effective member of the Constitution Party.

# How to Do It: Meetings

I believe that regular meetings are to be held, attendance taken, both annual membership fees and special contributions solicited, and training conducted to educate the members about the principles of the Constitution and the natural tendencies of those in authority to take power unto themselves. Only if we can defend the Constitution can we preserve it, for there are many who believe in a "living" Constitution and would gladly scrap in favor of one that contains many of the "rights" in place or being discussed today.

These monthly (or more frequent) meetings would run perhaps ninety minutes and be divided into three sections:

- Training
- Education
- Business

## *Training*

In the Training section we would discuss ways to recruit new members. Specifically, I have it in mind that members should be trained to canvass their neighborhoods. This is a very simple process. A member (or member and spouse, as appropriate, especially if both are members) go to a neighbor's home and ask if they could come in and talk to them for five minutes. They give a very quick but carefully written overview of the Constitution Party. They discuss why they are involved in it. They then invite their neighbors to come to a [monthly] meeting.

In this manner each member is not doing the actual recruiting. Five minutes is simply not enough time for anyone to make a good decision. Members *invite;* recruiters *recruit.* People must have an opportunity to see us "in action" and discover that we have common ground in our love of freedom and our support for the Constitution.

In the Training section we would also train current and future leaders of the organization regarding their duties and responsibilities. They need to know how to work with all types of people and to represent the organization properly.

Who would conduct the training? Those who have already received it and who have demonstrated their ability to conduct it.

## Education

The Education portion of the meeting would include streaming video or DVDs produced under the direction of the national leadership of the Constitution Party, and would include talks given by experts in various areas of the Constitution and experts on the issues of the day. Just as important, there ought to be reports given by members of the local group. This would be a lot like being back in school, for we would have homework. These reports could be book reviews or reports on assigned topics pertinent to the local area. The point is to give the members an opportunity to improve their public speaking skills and gain increased confidence in their ability to defend the Constitution.

Each member should be challenged to participate in a program of regular reading and study. It will be appropriate to provide a recommended reading list of books and articles for new members. Each local chapter could have its own schedule, and the recommended reading list could be prioritized. However, since we anticipate rapid growth of the organization, local needs will dictate the size of the list and the reading schedule.

It will be important to have members report on their reading. It is true that you cannot effectively teach something you do not fully understand. Giving a book report helps develop public speaking abilities, and enables members to gain confidence in their knowledge and understanding of the Constitution.

## Business

The Business section of the meeting would include a commitment or pledge made by each member. Nothing works unless people are willing to make a commitment and keep it. Today, hundreds of thousands of people who love the Constitution are asking themselves "What next?" This is what's next: the opportunity to get involved in an organization that has a mission statement, a purpose, and specific goals toward which it is working. I am absolutely certain that at least 1 million Americans, despite the current economic crisis, will be willing to make a financial commitment of $100 per year and one hour a week of their time.

The Business section would also involve planning for political activism similar to what is already happening but greatly expanded as this movement gains momentum. Each local "chapter" would be assigned the responsibility of maintaining contact with the local media, including press conferences (where appropriate), Letters to the Editor, interviews on radio and TV, and, of course, the Tea Parties.

As this organization grows, with strong leadership and with members who are growing every day in their confidence about the Constitution, exciting things will begin to happen. At some point the media will no longer be able to label us as they have so far, for they will have to take us seriously. I don't think it's impossible that the Constitution might even be taught in the public schools once again; we could certainly help to make that happen. As far as what's going on every day in Washington, we need to focus much more public attention on the Tenth amendment, States' Rights, and the unconstitutionality of almost all the legislation being passed by the Congress and signed by the President.

We should form alliances with numerous conservative groups including the Tea Party Patriots and the National Center for Constitutional Studies (NCCS). What a wonderful thing it would be to help them to expand their efforts to address groups all over the country and teach the principles of the Constitution.

# Typical Meetings

On a regular basis, two meetings should be held. One is the Executive Committee meeting, which is a business meeting in which the functioning of the organization is discussed and decisions made. In this meeting:

1. Candidates for office in the organization will be proposed, discussed, and decided upon.

2. Organization finances will be reviewed and decisions made regarding incoming and outgoing funds.

3. Fundraising will be discussed and projections made based upon current efforts.

4. Recruiting will be discussed and ways found to encourage members to bring more of their friends to meetings.

5. The agenda for the upcoming monthly regular meeting will be discussed and approved.

6. Training of leaders will be reviewed and appropriate decisions made.

7. The current education program will be reviewed and progress reported. Appropriate changes will be decided upon.

8. Key issues will be raised and decisions made regarding items of local interest being submitted to the national organization.

9. The campaign for action being sent from the national organization will be reviewed and discussed, and fitted to the local chapter and its members.

10. Political activism will be discussed and upcoming events considered or planned to promote the message.

# Regular [monthly] Meetings

The other meeting is the regular monthly meeting, divided into three thirty-minute segments with five-minute breaks. These meetings are very important, for in them we accomplish many of the purposes of this movement. The regular meetings should be carefully organized and conducted by those with adequate experience. Several chapter officers will serve during meetings, including:

| Officer | Time | Duties |
|---------|------|--------|
| Committee President or designee | Opening and Closing | Introduction and Dismissal |
| Trainer | Training segment | Conduct training |
| Teacher 1 | Training segment | Teach the Basic Course |
| Teacher 2 (assignment rotates among emembers) | Education segment | Teach the current material recommended by the Chapter leadership |
| Recruiter(s) | Business segment | Interview prospective members |
| Committee President or Designee | Business segment | Conduct business including administering the Pledge to new members |
| Activities Coordinator | Business segment | Schedules events in which members will participate, solicits support, and coordinates efforts |

| | | |
|---|---|---|
| Treasurer | Business segment | Gives financial reports (quarterly or as appropriate) |
| Parliamentarian (usually the Assistant Committee Chairman) | Business segment | Ensures that proper procedures are observed |

The first segment should be Training, during which those who are attending a meeting for the first time may be directed to the introductory class. In this class the basic principles of the Constitution will be taught, along with the writings of the Founding Fathers.

The second segment should be Education, at which all present will participate in the current class. These classes will have homework, including reading books and articles, participating in political activism, contacting elected officials, and discussing Constitutional principles with neighbors, friends, and coworkers. The classes should be taught on a rotating basis so that everyone gets a regular opportunity to teach. Teaching a class requires that the teacher be well prepared and promotes teaching and leadership skills that are vital to the organization.

Classes will include discussions of books read by assignment, writings of "experts" on issues of the day, and other important matters of interest. The goal is education rather than debate, but the Education portion of the meeting will be held at a higher level than the Basic course taught during the Training portion.

There will be lectures given by people at the National level (on streaming video or DVD) as well as from local members who have expertise in the various areas, but these lectures should not dominate the meeting or prevent all from participating in a meaningful way.

The Business portion of the meeting should be the last portion. At this time those who are willing to take the pledge will do so and make a real commitment to the cause of freedom. This should be handled with dignity and consideration, for each participant is important. Those not yet ready to make a commitment are welcome to sit in on the Business portion of the meeting to show that we have nothing to hide, and that what we are doing is intended to benefit all Americans by helping them appreciate freedom and natural rights.

In the Business portion announcements will be made regarding actions of the Executive committee. All members will be asked to sustain the decisions of the Executive Committee, and discussion will be permitted as appropriate. We must include all and alienate none both so that we may speak with one voice and that we may respect the worth of each member.

## Conducting the Regular Meetings

This is how a typical [monthly] meeting might be run (times are in hours/minutes):

| Time | Event 1 | Who Attends Event 1 | Event 2 | Who Attends Event 2 |
|------|---------|---------------------|---------|---------------------|
| 0:00 – 0:05 | Welcome, Announcements, and Introductions * | All attendees | - | - |
| 0:05 - 0:35 | Training (Party leadership training or Candidate training, as appropriate) | Those who have completed the Basic Course and invitees | Basic Constitution Course | New members and guests who have not completed the Basic Course |

| | | | | |
|---|---|---|---|---|
| 0:35 - 0:40 | Break | | | |
| 0:40 - 1:10 | Education | All attendees | - | - |
| 1:10 – 1:15 | Break | | | |
| 1:15 – 1:45 | Business | All except (see right) | Interviews | Those invited |
| 1:45-1:50 | Dismissal / Welcome to new members | All attendees | - | – |

*Brief opening and closing prayers are always appropriate in all meetings. After all, we are seeking God's help in restoring our country to its Constitutional foundation.

# The Pledge

I, _____, solemnly pledge my support to the Constitution of the United States to help restore America to its Constitutional foundation. I believe in freedom. I believe that faith, hard work, morality, integrity, and decency made America great and can do so again.

I commit a portion of my time, talents, and resources to this great work.

# The Commitment

Taking the Pledge makes a person a member of this movement. He or she will then begin to contribute one hundred dollars per year and a minimum of one hour per week to it. Some will immediately take the ball and run with it; others will need encouragement and help in living up to their promise. We need to act with wisdom and compassion to help all to progress, for all are needed and all can make their own unique contribution.

# The Process

Upon taking the Pledge, which should normally be done in the Business portion of a regular meeting, the new member will receive a specific assignment. He or she will be assigned to the New Member class to begin or complete the course before moving on to the more advanced classes. Prior to taking the Pledge the new member should have completed the *Talents and Abilities Survey* and been interviewed by a local leader. In that interview the leader and the prospective member will discuss the information on the Survey and determine where in the movement the new member should initially serve. Assignments will include committee memberships, teaching, organizing political activism, recruiting, and more.

# Fulfilling our Potential

We need not think in terms of whether we will succeed or fail. If we awaken just one person—ourselves—to the idea that we make ourselves free by our own efforts we will have succeeded. Participation in this movement will make people better. It will remind them of the duties of citizenship.

Throughout their history Americans have been famous for their religious faith, their hard work and diligence, their belief in the importance of improving themselves, their compassion and generosity, and the notion that we can be a great people. Though we have allowed ourselves to seek for lesser goals, many Americans still hold to the principles promoted by the Founding Fathers; it's just that many of them do not realize it, and many others believe that there is no political will to promote those things that made America great.

Millions of Americans will welcome the challenge to become better and to create something better than the status quo. We are still a people who possess faith in the future, and we have not lost the drive and initiative that once made us great. We must never doubt that we can return to our inspired Constitution. What once occurred through divine intervention can happen again through the same means. What we have to do is to help our fellow men and women become worthy of that miracle. We must deserve our freedom, or we will lose it. Even if we deserve it, freedom can be stolen from us through apathy and inaction on the part of the people in response to the unconstitutional actions of their elected officials. Allowing the many special interest groups and those who favor taking away our freedoms to establish a tyranny of the minority is not worthy of us. We must work very hard to reverse these tyrannies if we are to restore our freedoms.

Restoring America to its Constitutional foundation is worthy of the best in us. Aside from raising our family and instilling in our children a profound respect for the Constitution, one of the most important things we can do in life is to preserve those things we believe are given us by God. Clearly, the Constitution is one of the very few things worth fighting for. As we engage in this vital work, we will become better people. We will gain skills that will benefit us in every aspect of life. We will gain confidence in the future and lose the feeling of powerlessness from which so many Americans suffer. We will live better lives; we will be more honest, more chaste, more considerate in making decisions, more temperate, and more inclined to follow the Golden Rule.

As we work to defend the Constitution, we cannot help but look upon all men as brothers, for we will understand that under the law we are all equals. We do not live under the Constitution so that we may take advantage of one another; we live under this Constitution so that all may enjoy the blessings of freedom and prosper in accordance with our own God-given talents, abilities, and hard work.

## The (local or regional) Introductory Meeting

Since this program is new and, at this moment, untested, it is appropriate to introduce it on all three levels; at local chapters, state or regional meetings, and national meetings. Here are the purposes of such a meeting.

# Goal

To motivate Constitution Party members to adopt the program described in *The Patriots Guide to Taking America Back* as a means of greatly improving their recruitment and fundraising efforts.

# Objectives

1. Convince members that better organization will promote the Party's goals while helping members accomplish personal growth.
2. Help attendees better understand the scope and capabilities of the Constitution Party and its key role in the movement to return America to its Constitutional foundation.

# Strategies

1. Make the presentation in such a way as to appeal to people's integrity, ideals, and hopes for themselves and their families.

2. Utilize appropriate teaching methods to enlighten, educate, and convince attendees of the importance of this work and of each member.

# Plans

- Create meeting materials, flyers, and invitations.
- Invite specific groups and individuals with personal invitations as much as possible.
- Organize the meeting place and all components: seating, tables, sound, lighting, stage, props, banners, computers and projectors, writing materials, literature and items for sale, food, etc.
- Arrange for adequate help for setup, greeters, running the meeting, support staff, and teardown.

- Make all preparations: speakers, slide shows, handouts, etc.
- Conduct the meeting.
- Recruit new members.
- Administer the Pledge to new members.
- Close the meeting.
- Obtain feedback from participants.
- Incorporate feedback and constructive criticism into future meetings.

## Activities

| Event Duration | Cumulative Time | Item | Action / Who will perform |
|---|---|---|---|
| 6 min | 0:06 | Open the meeting | Greeting, opening prayer |
| 2 min | 0:08 | Introductions of Party officials, speakers, and honored guests | Local Chapter head |
| 2 min | 0:10 | Statement of Purpose | Local Chapter head |
| 60 min | 1:10 | Restoring the Constitution | Designated Teacher |
| 10 min | 1:20 | Break | |
| 40 min | 2:00 | Demonstrate a model local chapter meeting, including Education, Training, and Business | Invited Speaker |

| Event Duration | Cumulative Time | Item | Action / Who will perform |
|---|---|---|---|
| 8 min | Included above | Demonstrate a typical Basic Constitution Course class | Designated Teacher |
| 8 min | Included above | Demonstrate a typical Education class | Designated Teacher |
| 10 min | Included above | Demonstrate a Training session | Designated Trainer |
| 10 min | Included above | Demonstrate a Business meeting | Designated Speaker or local chapter head |
| 10 min | 2:10 | Break | |
| 10 min | 2:20 | Demonstrate interviews of prospective members | Designated Recruiter |
| 5 min | 2:25 | Describe the requirements of membership in the local chapter of the CP | Designated Speaker |
| 5 min | 2:30 | Describe the basic beliefs and platform of the Constitution Party | Designated Speaker |
| 5 min | 2:35 | Invite all present to take the Pledge | Local Chapter head |

| Event Duration | Cumulative Time | Item | Action / Who will perform |
|---|---|---|---|
| 5 min | 2:40 | Administer the Pledge | Local Chapter head |
| 10 min | 2:50 | Discuss the Party's local and national goals | Designated Speaker |
| 10 min | 3:00 | Closing / Thanks / Closing Prayer | Local Chapter head |
| At the close of the meeting provide New Member materials and receive or arrange to receive annual contributions from new members. | | | |
| 30 min | 3:30 | Lunch / teardown | |

- Conduct the meeting.
- Recruit new members.
- Administer the Pledge to new members.
- Close the meeting.
- Obtain feedback from participants.
- Incorporate feedback and constructive criticism into future meetings.

# Afterword

The task of writing The *Patriots Guide to Taking America Back* has not been an easy one. I undertook this project after I attended a National Committee meeting of the Constitution Party in Newark, New Jersey, in the spring of 2009. It was there that I met Howard Phillips for the first time, and I expressed to him my disappointment at finding the Constitution Party to be what I later described as "comatose." Howard is the founder of both the Conservative Caucus and the Constitution Party, and has been of great assistance to the conservative movement for many years.

Howard asked me what I was going to do about it. My career has been devoted to helping Americans do better financially. Over a span of thirty years, my work had changed. It now has just as much to do with defending my clients against an aggressive central government as it does with managing their investments. I have seen many of our constitutional guarantees of freedom stripped away from us, including our privacy, our freedom from self-incrimination, our property rights, and much more. I began to feel that there was little point in working hard to make money for someone if the government was going to take it all away.

It was time to make a decision. I continue to fight for my clients as I strive to create wealth for them and to help them preserve it from inflation, taxes, and the declining dollar. Because of what our government has done to us, that pursuit becomes more hopeless every day. My next book, which will be titled *What Will You Do When the Money's No Good?*, will discuss what I am firmly convinced will be the ultimate demise of the dollar, possibly within the next ten years. If I am right, when the dollar disappears, this country, and indeed our entire world, will experience great upheaval. Much, and even most of the wealth I have created for my clients in more than thirty years will be wiped out unless I can find ways for them to preserve what they have in vehicles other than those denominated in dollars. My career in personal financial planning is changing into a desperate effort to help my clients and others save themselves.

That was my initial response to Howard's challenge. He then said that "one excuse is good as any other," and that ended the conversation. It didn't take long for me to realize that I had given him a very poor answer, and if every American were to give a similar lame response such as the more popular "I'm too busy," our constitutional republic would indeed fail, and Americans would become slaves to the welfare state—or worse.

I have written and published my *Wealth Creation and Preservation* newsletter for more than seventeen years. My first book, *Moneywise: Your Guide to Keeping Ahead of Inflation, Taxes, and the Declining Dollar,* was written to help alert hundreds of thousands of Americans to what their government, the media, and Wall Street were doing to them, and to enable them to take charge of their own personal finances before it was too late. Though I minored in Political Science at the State University of New York at Stony Brook, I had not been politically involved since Ronald Reagan left office. If I was going to get involved in defending the Constitution I needed to know more—much more.

I got involved with the Augusta County chapter of the Constitution Party and developed a pilot program by which I hoped to restructure the Party in such a way as to help it fulfill its purpose and bring it many new members. I became more involved in the Constitution Party on a national level as well, and began to get invitations to speak in various parts of the United States. All of this was done at my own expense. At each speaking engagement I tried to solicit the opinions and ideas of those in attendance so that I could find out how much they knew about the Constitution, how well they understood it, how committed they were to defending the Constitution, and what made them different from those who were not involved in the Constitution Party.

This volume is the result. It is a work in progress, and I hope to have a second and even a third edition available over the next several years. Like the Constitution, this book is an experiment. The purpose of the experiment is to awaken the American people to a sense of their responsibilities as citizens of our Republic, and to motivate them to get educated and to get involved politically as they always should have been, but with one great difference. Since the majority of the critical issues that face us today have to do with wealth redistribution, social engineering, and morality, what must be done is to help many Americans find the spiritual and moral foundation for their lives.

If this "experiment" fails, the Constitution will fail, and the United States will probably end up being merged into some North American Union. The greatest government in the history of our planet will have been discarded, and we all will be responsible.

By now you have noticed that I have avoided most of the details regarding the leading issues of our day in my discussion of the problems facing us. All of us need to look at the bigger picture, which is the constant conflict between freedom and slavery. Freedom has been losing the battle all over the world. It's almost as if Americans, witnessing the fall of the Soviet Union and the changes to China subsequent to the Cultural Revolution, declared victory in the establishment of freedom and fell fast asleep.

We cannot allow ourselves to be distracted by the details, or by who said what to whom. We need to join the battle on the side of freedom, and we should have done so years ago. We don't even need to be angry at those who in many cases have deliberately robbed us of our freedoms or bought us off with empty promises. Anger only wastes our time and energy, and we need a great deal of both if we are to have any hope of success.

# My personal plea to all Americans

Please read the Constitution. Talk to people who know and understand the Constitution better than you do and who love and respect it. Develop an appreciation for this sacred document and for those who brought it forth upon the face of the earth. Learn what it means for government to act in a constitutional manner. Then, examine what's going on in our world in light of your new understanding of the Constitution. You will begin to see the great inconsistencies between the actions of government and the intentions of the Founding Fathers. Over time, you will develop a deeper understanding of how far we have moved away from the Constitution.

As you begin this educational process you also need to get involved. There is today in the United States a Constitution Party. This party, like every other political party, was established in order to do the things the political parties do: to get candidates of a certain political leaning elected to public office and to try to impose its platform upon the American people. Neither of the major parties today has a Constitutional platform; both parties have been "hijacked" by special-interest groups, individuals, and organizations which have imposed their own agendas in exchange for their votes.

As I have detailed in the preceding pages, my vision of the Constitution Party is quite different from that of the political parties in power today. I would like to see the Constitution Party be one place where Americans can vote their consciences. At the same time, I would like to see the Constitution Party promote a platform that is entirely consistent with the Constitution itself and with the intentions of the Founding Fathers.

When you became a Republican or a Democrat, you did not sign a pledge to vote the party line in every election for the rest of your life. The same is true of the Constitution Party. In a perfect world, all Americans would vote for the best candidate after carefully examining the issues and the candidates, but this is not a perfect world. The Constitution Party will, it is hoped and expected, run only those candidates who have made a firm commitment to sustain and defend the Constitution of the United States. This commitment is identical to that which is taken by elected officials at almost every level of government throughout the United States, but it is ignored by the vast majority of them. This is why morality, integrity, and decency are so vital in the political arena, for those who have taken that oath and then ignored it are the same people who are destroying the Constitution and this country.

We all remember the *USS Arizona,* the mighty battleship sunk by the Japanese during the attack on Pearl Harbor on December 7, 1941. For years the Arizona had been a symbol of American power and prestige and sailed the world's oceans as an ambassador of goodwill—though more on the order of "speak softly and carry a big stick." The ship was commissioned in 1913 and never saw real action prior to Pearl Harbor Day, though it served many purposes over a period of almost three decades.

One thousand, one hundred and seventy-seven Navy seamen and officers lost their lives aboard the Arizona on Pearl Harbor Day. Hundreds were trapped below decks as the ship began to sink. As seawater flooded into below-decks compartments, the amount of available air rapidly diminished. Imagine yourself in such a predicament, trapped in a steel compartment with no means of escape and water rapidly rising to the ceiling. That's where the American people are today. Because we have slept while our government seized more and more power, the "water"—the welfare state and tyranny—is rising rapidly, and we and our country are about to drown in a sea of debt, corruption, greed, and the lust for power.

The "water" is rising. The "window" of escape—the right to speak out, to remove corrupt elected officials, and to repeal this mountain of bad legislation, Executive Orders, and court rulings—is almost closed. It may not be very long now—perhaps a matter of months at best—before the only course open to those who love America is armed rebellion. That would be a terrible waste of good lives.

I have made a commitment to spend some time every day for the rest of my life in the struggle to defend and preserve the Constitution of the United States and our republic. I don't do this to seek for wealth or the praise of men. I do it because it is what all who love freedom should do.

Will you join me?

# Appendix

## Interviews

My leadership experience over the past thirty years has convinced me that interviews are essential. I believe that all organizations can benefit from carefully planned and properly conducted interviews. Let me share with you some reasons for my beliefs.

Americans are great "joiners," but we often lack the initiative and motivation to stay the course and see the job through. It is easier to say we will do something than it is to actually do it. In a proper interview we are given the opportunity to select goals for our participation in the organization for which we are being interviewed. These goals have power; they motivate us because they are things *we* have decided we want to do. In addition, our goals are integrated with those of others and become the goals the organization will accomplish.

How does this happen? It happens because in a good interview we have the opportunity to talk about ourselves and to review our own lives and our experiences, our feelings, and our beliefs. We share things about ourselves with someone who should be genuinely interested in us, not only as members of an organization, but as human beings.

Most of us have very few opportunities to share ourselves with others in this way and to have someone who is interested in us help us see ourselves in a true light. This is especially true in the twenty-first century, when millions of people have hundreds of acquaintances but very few real friends. A century ago, Americans would participate in large groups in a wide variety of activities including public events and observances, festivals, bazaars, fairs, sporting events, religious observances, and other activities in our communities.

Some of these activities remain to this day, but the level of participation is a fraction of what it used to be. Television and other entertainment, divorce, drug abuse, alcoholism, pornography, video games, political polarization, rising dishonesty, and so many other things tend to keep people apart and prevent us from forming the close relationships that are so vitally important to a moral and productive society. We can be lonely in Times Square on New Year's Eve because we do not have the comfortable feeling we used to enjoy when we were in the company of our fellow Americans.

Today we have support groups and rehab clinics and reality TV. None of these is an appropriate substitute for friendship, affection, or duty. We have many things to worry about, and often it may seem that there is no one to share our burdens with us. Have you ever wanted to just sit down with someone you felt you could trust and who was interested in you, and talk about the things that were on your mind? Millions of Americans have felt exactly that way.

Now, one interview is not going to enable you to solve all of your problems or anyone else's. An interview has a specific purpose, and the successful interview accomplishes that purpose. Here are some of the things an interview can accomplish:

- Create a relationship of trust between the interviewer and the interviewee.

- Give the interviewee an opportunity to talk about him or herself in a one-on-one environment.

- Promote the sharing of ideas.

- Encourage the interviewee to examine his or her own life and consider the direction it is going.

- Enable the interviewee to understand the purpose of personal goals, to help the interviewee set his or her own goals, and to motivate the interviewee to work toward and achieve the goals thus created.

- Explain the purpose of the interview and the purpose of the organization, and what role the interviewee might play if he or she were to become a member and an active participant.

- Ask the interviewee if he or she agrees that the purposes of the organization are worthwhile and appropriate. If so, ask if he or she is willing to make some personal sacrifices to help the Party fulfill its goals.

- Share the organization's goals and mission statement, and enable the interviewee to personally "catch the vision."

- Determine whether the interviewee is an appropriate candidate for the organization.

- Extend an invitation for the interviewee to join and participate in the organization.

All of us want to be listened to. We want our ideas and opinions to matter to someone besides ourselves. An interview can but does not necessarily include counseling. A good interview should be uplifting to both participants. Used effectively, interviews can help build and strengthen an organization while it helps its members to accomplish personal growth.

## Conducting Interviews

If we were merely trying to recruit people to vote for a candidate or to participate in a protest meeting, we would probably not need to interview them. However, we are asking people to make a long-term commitment of time, talents, and resources. They have every right to know what may be expected of them before they make such a commitment.

For example, each prospective member should attend at least one set of meetings before being recruited so that they may meet our members, find out how we operate, and make a decision as to whether they wish to participate in the defense of freedom. Their interview will give them an opportunity to learn the complete list of expectations and requirements they will be asked to agree to. Ours is a voluntary organization; we compel no one to serve or even to attend. If we cannot persuade by our works that we belong to something worthwhile, we deserve to see prospective members turn away.

A good interview cannot be faked. The interviewer must be sincere, genuinely interested in the person he is interviewing, kind, compassionate, and understanding. After all, we are going to ask our members and prospective members to give up some of their beliefs in exchange for others. The Constitution Party is 100 percent pro-life and pro-Constitution. Constitution Party members are expected to hold to high moral standards that are self-imposed. We must set an example of appropriate conduct, decency, and integrity in every situation. In addition, we must learn much if we hope to be able to properly defend our Constitution. That's a lot to ask of anyone; it is almost miraculous that so many are willing to try.

In a counseling environment you might expect to visit one-on-one with the interviewer. That way you maintain complete privacy, for only two people are involved. In the Constitution Party, we may feel free to interview husband and wife together. If both spouses are interested in defending the cause of freedom they will support each other in their efforts.

In these interviews we will not probe for human weaknesses or negative psychological attributes; instead, we are looking for a genuine desire to serve, a love of country, a willingness to teach others, and a level of humility that can keep us going despite what others may say about us. In one sense we are building a team, one that will compete in the most important game in history. We must be capable of working together and being united in our understanding and respect for the principles we espouse.

How do we accomplish this in an interview? Let's take a look at a hypothetical interview of an individual who is a prospective member. Please note that we use no "tricks," "sales techniques," or pressure to get people to join us. We have no right to do that when we are working with volunteers, particularly when we are asking them to serve in this great cause. There will be no criticisms, no browbeating, no psychological games, nothing that will make the interviewee feel uncomfortable or cause him to distrust us.

## A Hypothetical Situation

This individual is in his thirties. He is male, a blue-collar worker, he finished high school, he has been active in the Tea Party movement, his political leaning is Libertarian, and he has the usual concerns about being able to provide for his family. We'll call him Gary.

### *The Interview*

The interviewer greets Gary after the Education and Training sections of the regular meeting. They go into a separate room where they will be undisturbed. Here is their conversation:

Interviewer: Thank you for attending our meeting today. As I mentioned, I am a recruiter for this local chapter of the Constitution Party. That means that I have the privilege of meeting with people like you who are concerned about the direction our country is taking. Let me put you at ease. I will ask you some questions as we talk about the Party and about you. You are under no obligation to answer any of them. All information you give me will remain strictly confidential, and will not be shared with anyone without your consent. The purpose of this visit is to help you understand who we are and what we hope to accomplish. It will also help us determine where you might best be able to assist us in restoring America to its Constitutional foundation.

Is this the first time you have attended a Constitution Party meeting?

| | |
|---|---|
| Gary: | Yes. I have been invited several times but have had a hard time freeing up an evening to attend. |
| Interviewer: | What are your initial impressions? |
| Gary: | I've never seen anything like this. I expected something quite different. |
| Interviewer: | What did you expect? |
| Gary: | I guess I expected more of a political rally than an educational program. I suppose I haven't seen very much of what you do yet. |
| Interviewer: | You're right. These meetings are very specific in their purpose. Most of what we do takes place outside of these meetings. Here we are trying to teach one another and learn about the principles of freedom so that we can be more effective in accomplishing our objectives. We will talk about them in a moment. First, tell me a little about yourself. |
| Gary: | Like many people I know, I believe our government has made some mistakes and that instead of helping us they are hurting us. It seems to me that our elected officials don't listen to us. I have been involved in the Libertarian Party, and I supported Ron Paul in the election in 2008, but I never got involved in politics prior to that time. My work keeps me going as much as fifty hours a week, and what free time I have I usually spend with my family. |
| | I work hard, and I am concerned that taxes are too high. I worry that my children will have to pay the debts we are creating now. I want to provide a better life for them, if I can. |

| | |
|---|---|
| Interviewer: | Thank you for sharing that. If you don't mind, I would like to take some notes. They are my own property and are not shared with anyone else. |
| Gary: | That's okay. |
| Interviewer: | How well do you understand the Constitution? |
| Gary: | To be honest, I don't remember much of what I learned about it in school. I would like to know more. |
| Interviewer: | Do you have any experience in writing or public speaking? |
| Gary: | No. |
| Interviewer: | Do you believe that honest people can bring about positive change? In other words, do you believe that you could work with people who feel the way you do to make our country better for you and your family? |
| Gary: | I think so. I just don't know what to do. |
| Interviewer: | We think so too. That's why all of us are here. What thoughts do you have about how we could bring back the freedoms are guaranteed by the Constitution, which have been taken away by our government? |
| Gary: | I hadn't thought about it like that. Some of my friends write to their congressmen from time to time, and several people I know went to Washington to participate in the big rally. I suppose we could get involved more in local elections, but most of the time it doesn't seem like we really know much about the candidates. The issues that our leaders talk about and work on seem to be very complex, and they are difficult to understand. I know what I'd like to see, but I really don't know how to go about it. |

Interviewer: What would you like to see?

Gary: I like our schools to be better so that my children could get a good education that would prepare them for college and for a career. I'd like to not feel that I'm being lied to all the time by politicians. I'd like to save for retirement, and I'd like my money to go further than it does. I wish I didn't have to work so many hours and be away from my family so much of the time.

Interviewer: We all share those concerns and would like the same things for ourselves and our families. We believe that if more Americans stood up for the things that they wanted, this would be a better country.

May I take a look at the Talents and Abilities Survey that you completed for us?

Gary: Sure.

Interviewer: Do you enjoy what you do for a living?

Gary: I like what I do. Someday I'd like to run my own company, but I'm glad I don't with this recession we've got right now.

Interviewer: You mentioned that you don't have any experience in writing or public speaking. Have your been asked to teach a Sunday school class or provide some training for your fellow employees?

Gary: A couple of times my bosses sent me to a class for training, and when I came back I shared some of what I had learned with the guys in my shop.

Interviewer: Is that something that you are comfortable with or feel you could become comfortable with?

Gary: I knew the material pretty well because it was still fresh in my mind, but I've never been really comfortable standing in front of a group of people.

Interviewer: You had confidence in your ability to share the information because it was fresh in your mind, but you hadn't been given any training as to how to teach it. Do you think you could teach a class if you were taught a little bit about how to teach?

Gary: I think I could. I'd be willing to try.

Interviewer: That's all we ask for. If people are willing to try, we will do all that we can to train them and help them to feel comfortable in doing the things they are asked to do.

Let's review the purpose of the Constitution Party and what we hope to accomplish as we work in the cause of freedom. (The interviewer then proceeds to discuss briefly the basic principles and platform of the Constitution Party and then shares the Party's vision of its important work and what we hope to accomplish.)

Gary, all of us are volunteers. No one pays us for the work that we do. We believe in what we do, and we willingly give up our time, talents, and means to move this great work along. We are hopeful that millions of Americans will join us as they learn to love freedom as much as we do. You have taken an important step by coming to our meeting today. I appreciate the things that you have shared with me, and I believe that you could make a positive contribution to this work. I invite you to become a member of the Constitution party and take the pledge. If you accept this invitation, we will expect you to do several things:

- Engage in daily personal study of the Constitution and the writings of the Founding Fathers.

- Attend all the regularly scheduled meetings of this local Committee of the Constitution Party. We realize that sometimes circumstances prevent us from attending, but we'd like you to make these meetings a regular event and put them on your calendar well in advance.

- Contribute a minimum of $100 per year to the Constitution party to help us in this work.

- Receive training from us to prepare you to serve in the party as an officer or a teacher and to help you invite your friends and neighbors to attend meetings with you. You were invited here today by one of our members, and we expect you to do the same.

- You may expect to be asked to serve as an officer or a teacher in the Party, or to be given a specific assignment involving political activism or a number of different activities that are conducted by the Party.

- You may even be asked if you would be willing to run for elective office. We always need good people who take seriously their oath of office, and who are knowledgeable about the Constitution and all the laws that they swear to uphold.

- Finally, we ask you to actively participate with us and share your ideas. If you are concerned about something the Party intends to do, be sure to discuss it with me or with one of the other Committee officers. It's never easy to bring dozens of independently minded people together and get them working in a common cause, but that is exactly what we must do.

|               | Are you ready to make a decision today, or would you like to think about it and give us your answer within one week? |
|---------------|---|
| Gary:         | I would like to get involved, and I think I'm ready to become a member right now. As long as you are going to help me learn about the Constitution I think I might be able to help. |
| Interviewer:  | Thank you for giving me an opportunity to visit with you. I would like you to complete this application for membership now, and in just a few minutes we will go into the business portion of our meeting, and you will have the opportunity to take the pledge. Please make sure that you get your reading assignment from our Basic class teacher _____ so that you'll be prepared for our next meeting which will be on _____ |

## A Recap: What actually happened?

In this interview, several things happened. First, you will notice that the interviewer interspersed closed-ended and open-ended questions in order to properly direct the conversation. The interviewer did his best to put the interviewee at ease. He asked permission to take notes and told him that those notes would not be shared with anyone without his knowledge. He invited him to talk about himself and the things that were important to him.

The interviewer did three very important things; he asked, he listened, and he learned about the person he was interviewing. He was obviously interested in the person he was talking to. For many people, having someone show that kind of interest is like a breath of fresh air. Most of us tend to keep things that are personal to us "bottled up" inside—except, of course, for those who are addicted to Facebook and other "social media"—

because they're things that are personal to us that we feel others would not consider as important as we do.

Being able to share ideas and the innermost feelings of our hearts in a non-threatening environment with someone who is genuinely interested in us can be an extremely pleasant experience. The idea that "no one cares how much you know until they know how much you care" applies here. Being given the opportunity to share things that are important to us also puts us into a frame of mind where we are more receptive to the thoughts and ideas of others. We are more likely to want to get involved when we know that people care about us.

This interview would close when a commitment has been made by the person being interviewed. Without being pressured, this individual or couple will have set a personal goal to become involved and active in the Constitution Party and made at least a mental commitment of their time, talents, and resources to the Party and to the cause of the Constitution. Alternatively, they may have made a commitment to come back to the next meeting to see how they feel after a little more exposure to the Party and the way it works. Either way, they should never feel under any obligation, though we want to make sure that everyone we talk to understands the great importance of our personal involvement in restoring the Constitution. Millions of loyal Americans are needed to bring us back, and each deserves to have his or her ideas and opinions respected. Each of them also needs to know how much they are needed.

# Not Yours to Give

One day in the House of Representatives, a bill was taken up appropriating money for the benefit of a widow of a distinguished naval officer. Several beautiful speeches had been made in its support. The Speaker was just about to put the question when Crockett arose:

"Mr. Speaker—I have as much respect for the memory of the deceased, and as much sympathy for the sufferings of the living, if suffering there be, as any man in this House, but we must not permit our respect for the dead or our sympathy for a part of the living to lead us into an act of injustice to the balance of the living. I will not go into an argument to prove that Congress has no power to appropriate this money as an act of charity. Every member upon this floor knows it. We have the right, as individuals, to give away as much of our own money as we please in charity; but as members of Congress, we have no right so to appropriate a dollar of the public money. Some eloquent appeals have been made to us upon the ground that it is a debt due the deceased. Mr. Speaker, the deceased lived long after the close of the war; he was in office to the day of his death, and I have never heard that the government was in arrears to him.

Every man in this House knows it is not a debt. We cannot, without the grossest corruption, appropriate this money as the payment of a debt. We have not the semblance of authority to appropriate it as a charity. Mr. Speaker, I have said we have the right to give as much money of our own as we please. I am the poorest man on this floor. I cannot vote for this bill, but I will give one week's pay to the object, and if every member of Congress will do the same, it will amount to more than the bill asks."

He took his seat. Nobody replied. The bill was put upon its passage, and, instead of passing unanimously, as was generally supposed, and as, no doubt, it would, but for that speech, it received but few votes, and, of course, was lost.

Later, when asked by a friend why he had opposed the appropriation, Crockett gave this explanation:

•••

Several years ago, I was one evening standing on the steps of the Capitol with some other members of Congress, when our attention was attracted by a great light over in Georgetown. It was evidently a large fire. We jumped into a hack and drove over as fast as we could. In spite of all that could be done, many houses were burned and many families made homeless, and besides, some of them had lost all but the clothes they had on. The weather was very cold, and when I saw so many women and children suffering, I felt that something ought to be done for them. The next morning a bill was introduced appropriating $20,000 for their relief. We put aside all other business and rushed it through as soon as it could be done.

The next summer, when it began to be time to think about the election, I concluded I would take a scout around among the boys of my district. I had no opposition there, but, as the election was some time off, I did not know what might turn up. When riding one day in a part of my district in which I was more of a stranger than any other, I saw a man in a field plowing and coming toward the road. I gauged my gait so that we should meet as he came to the fence. As he came up, I spoke to the man. He replied politely, but, as I thought, rather coldly.

I began: "Well, friend, I am one of those unfortunate beings called 'candidates,' and—"

"Yes, I know you; you are Colonel Crockett, I have seen you once before, and voted for you the last time you were elected. I suppose you are out electioneering now, but you had better not waste your time or mine. I shall not vote for you again."

This was a sockdolager ... I begged him to tell me what was the matter.

"Well, Colonel, it is hardly worthwhile to waste time or words upon it. I do not see how it can be mended, but you gave a vote last winter which shows that either you have not capacity to understand the Constitution, or that you are wanting in the honesty and firmness to be guided by it. In either case, you are not the man to represent me. But I beg your pardon for expressing it in that way. I did not intend to avail myself of the privilege of the constituent to speak plainly to a candidate for the purpose of insulting or wounding you. I intend by it only to say that your understanding of the Constitution is very different from mine; and I will say to you what, but for my rudeness, I should not have said, that I believe you to be honest ... But an understanding of the Constitution different from mine I cannot overlook, because the Constitution, to be worth anything, must be held sacred, and rigidly observed in all its provisions. The man who wields power and misinterprets it is the more dangerous the more honest he is."

"I admit the truth of all you say, but there must be some mistake about it, for I do not remember that I gave any vote last winter upon any constitutional question."

"No, Colonel, there's no mistake. Though I live here in the backwoods and seldom go from home, I take the papers from Washington and read very carefully all the proceedings of Congress. My papers say that last winter you voted for a bill to appropriate $20,000 to some sufferers by a fire in Georgetown. Is that true?"

"Well, my friend, I may as well own up. You have got me there. But certainly nobody will complain that a great and rich country like ours should give the insignificant sum of $20,000 to relieve its suffering women and children, particularly with a full and overflowing Treasury, and I am sure, if you had been there, you would have done just as I did."

"It is not the amount, Colonel, that I complain of; it is the principle. In the first place, the government ought to have in the Treasury no more than enough for its legitimate purposes. But that has nothing to do with the question. The power of collecting and disbursing money at pleasure is the most dangerous power that can be entrusted to man, particularly under our system of collecting revenue by a tariff, which reaches every man in the country, no matter how poor he may be, and the poorer he is the more he pays in proportion to his means. What is worse, it presses upon him without his knowledge where the weight centers, for there is not a man in the United States who can ever guess how much he pays to the government. So you see, while you are contributing to relieve one, you are drawing it from thousands who are even worse off than he. If you had the right to give anything, the amount was simply a matter of discretion with you, and you had as much right to give $20,000,000 as $20,000. If you have the right to give to one, you have the right to give to all; and, as the Constitution neither defines charity nor stipulates the amount, you are at liberty to give to any and everything which you may believe, or profess to believe, is a charity, and to any amount you may think proper. You will very easily perceive what a wide door this would open for fraud and corruption and favoritism, on the one hand, and for robbing the people on the other. No, Colonel, Congress has no right to give charity. Individual members may give as much of their own money as they please, but they have no right to touch a dollar of the public money for that purpose. If twice as many houses had been burned in this county as in Georgetown, neither you nor any other member of Congress would have thought of appropriating a dollar for our relief. There are about two hundred and forty members of Congress. If they had shown their sympathy for the sufferers by contributing each one week's pay, it would have made over $13,000. There are plenty of wealthy men in and around Washington who could have given $20,000 without depriving themselves of even a luxury of life. The congressmen chose to keep their own money, which, if reports be true, some of them spend not very creditably; and the people about Washington, no doubt, applauded you for relieving them from the necessity of giving by giving what was not yours to give. The people have delegated to Congress, by the Constitution, the power to do certain things. To do these, it is authorized to collect and pay moneys, and for nothing else. Everything beyond this is usurpation, and a violation of the Constitution.

"So you see, Colonel, you have violated the Constitution in what I consider a vital point. It is a precedent fraught with danger to the country, for when Congress once begins to stretch its power beyond the limits of the Constitution, there is no limit to it, and no security for the people. I have no doubt you acted honestly, but that does not make it any better, except as far as you are personally concerned, and you see that I cannot vote for you."

I tell you I felt streaked. I saw if I should have opposition, and this man should go to talking, he would set others to talking, and in that district I was a gone fawn-skin. I could not answer him, and the fact is, I was so fully convinced that he was right, I did not want to. But I must satisfy him, and I said to him:

"Well, my friend, you hit the nail upon the head when you said I had not sense enough to understand the Constitution. I intended to be guided by it, and thought I had studied it fully. I have heard many speeches in Congress about the powers of Congress, but what you have said here at your plow has got more hard, sound sense in it than all the fine speeches I ever heard. If I had ever taken the view of it that you have, I would have put my head into the fire before I would have given that vote; and if you will forgive me and vote for me again, if I ever vote for another unconstitutional law I wish I may be shot."

He laughingly replied, "Yes, Colonel, you have sworn to that once before, but I will trust you again upon one condition. You say that you are convinced that your vote was wrong. Your acknowledgment of it will do more good than beating you for it. If, as you go around the district, you will tell people about this vote, and that you are satisfied it was wrong, I will not only vote for you, but will do what I can to keep down opposition, and, perhaps, I may exert some little influence in that way."

"If I don't," said I, "I wish I may be shot; and to convince you that I am in earnest in what I say I will come back this way in a week or ten days, and if you will get up a gathering of the people, I will make a speech to them. Get up a barbecue, and I will pay for it."

"No, Colonel, we are not rich people in this section, but we have plenty of provisions to contribute for a barbecue, and some to spare for those who have none. The push of crops will be over in a few days, and we can then afford a day for a barbecue. This is Thursday; I will see to getting it up on Saturday week. Come to my house on Friday, and we will go together, and I promise you a very respectable crowd to see and hear you."

"Well, I will be here. But one thing more before I say goodbyee. I must know your name."

"My name is Bunce."

"Not Horatio Bunce?"

"Yes."

"Well, Mr. Bunce, I never saw you before, though you say you have seen me, but I know you very well. I am glad I have met you, and very proud that I may hope to have you for my friend."

It was one of the luckiest hits of my life that I met him. He mingled but little with the public, but was widely known for his remarkable intelligence and incorruptible integrity, and for a heart brimful and running over with kindness and benevolence, which showed themselves not only in words but in acts. He was the oracle of the whole country around him, and his fame had extended far beyond the circle of his immediate acquaintance. Though I had never met him before, I had heard much of him, and but for this meeting it is very likely I should have had opposition, and had been beaten. One thing is very certain, no man could now stand up in that district under such a vote.

At the appointed time I was at his house, having told our conversation to every crowd I had met, and to every man I stayed all night with, and I found that it gave the people an interest and a confidence in me stronger than I had every seen manifested before.

Though I was considerably fatigued when I reached his house, and, under ordinary circumstances, should have gone early to bed, I kept him up until midnight, talking about the principles and affairs of government, and got more real, true knowledge of them than I had got all my life before.

I have known and seen much of him since, for I respect him—no, that is not the word—I reverence and love him more than any living man, and I go to see him two or three times every year; and I will tell you, sir, if every one who professes to be a Christian lived and acted and enjoyed it as he does, the religion of Christ would take the world by storm.

But to return to my story. The next morning we went to the barbecue, and, to my surprise, found about a thousand men there. I met a good many whom I had not known before, and they and my friend introduced me around until I had got pretty well acquainted—at least, they all knew me.

In due time notice was given that I would speak to them. They gathered up around a stand that had been erected. I opened my speech by saying:

"Fellow citizens—I present myself before you today feeling like a new man. My eyes have lately been opened to truths which ignorance or prejudice, or both, had heretofore hidden from my view. I feel that I can today offer you the ability to render you more valuable service than I have ever been able to render before. I am here today more for the purpose of acknowledging my error than to seek your votes. That I should make this acknowledgment is due to myself as well as to you. Whether you will vote for me is a matter for your consideration only."

I went on to tell them about the fire and my vote for the appropriation and then told them why I was satisfied it was wrong. I closed by saying:

"And now, fellow citizens, it remains only for me to tell you that the most of the speech you have listened to with so much interest was simply a repetition of the arguments by which your neighbor, Mr. Bunce, convinced me of my error."

It is the best speech I ever made in my life, but he is entitled to the credit for it. And now I hope he is satisfied with his convert and that he will get up here and tell you so.

He came upon the stand and said:

"Fellow citizens, it affords me great pleasure to comply with the request of Colonel Crockett. I have always considered him a thoroughly honest man, and I am satisfied that he will faithfully perform all that he has promised you today."

He went down, and there went up from that crowd such a shout for Davy Crockett as his name never called forth before.

I am not much given to tears, but I was taken with a choking then and felt some big drops rolling down my cheeks. And I tell you now that the remembrance of those few words spoken by such a man, and the honest, hearty shout they produced, is worth more to me than all the honors I have received and all the reputation I have ever made, or ever shall make, as a member of Congress.

"Now, sir," concluded Crockett, "you know why I made that speech yesterday.

There is one thing now to which I will call your attention. You remember that I proposed to give a week's pay. There are in that House many very wealthy men—men who think nothing of spending a week's pay, or a dozen of them, for a dinner or a wine party when they have something to accomplish by it. Some of those same men made beautiful speeches upon the great debt of gratitude which the country owed the deceased—a debt which could not be paid by money—and the insignificance and worthlessness of money, particularly so insignificant a sum as $10,000, when weighted against the honor of the nation. Yet not one of them responded to my proposition. Money with them is nothing but trash when it is to come out of the people. But it is the one great thing for which most of them are striving, and many of them sacrifice honor, integrity, and justice to obtain it."

This edition of *Not Yours to Give* was taken, with appreciation, from the Web site for the Foundation for Economics Education, www.fee.org.

# Bibliography

In all instances I try to find books written without bias or prejudice in favor of one political philosophy or another. At the same time, this list must include books favorable to the Constitution and to the thinking of the Founding Fathers.

## The Constitution

*The U.S. Constitution and Fascinating Facts About It,* Oak Hill Publishing Company, 2009. www.constitutionfacts.com .

Ackerrman, Bruce, *The Failure of the Founding Fathers: Jefferson, Marshall, and the Rise of Presidential Democracy,* The Belknap Press of Harvard University Press, 2005

Fineman, Howard, *The 13 American Arguments: Enduring Debates That Define and Inspire Our Country,* Random House, 2008

Hamilton, Alexander, Madison, James, and John Jay, *The Federalist Papers,* Bantam Books, 1982

Jefferson, Thomas, *Notes on the State of Virginia,* University Of North Carolina Press, 1982

Lipsky, Seth, *The Citizen's Constitution: An Annotated Guide,* Basic Books, 2009

McDonald, Forrest, *States' Rights and the Union: Imperium in Imperio, 1776–1876,* University press of Kansas, 2000.

Padover, Saul K., *The Living U.S. Constitution,* Third Revised Edition, Meridian, 1995

Peters, William, *A More Perfect Union: The Making of the United States Constitution,* Crown Publishers, 1987.

Skousen, W. Cleon, *The Five Thousand Year Leap: The 28 Ideas That Changed the World,* National Center for Constitutional Studies 1981

Story, Joseph, *A Familiar Exposition of the Constitution of the United States,* Regnery, 1986

## American History

Beeman, Richard, *Plain, Honest Men: The Making of the American Constitution,* Random House, 2009

Davis, David Brion, and Mintz, Steven, *The Boisterous Sea of Liberty: A Documentary History of America from Discovery Through the Civil War,* Oxford University Press, 1998

Ellis, Joseph J., *Founding Brothers: The Revolutionary Generation,* Vintage Books, 2002.

Ellis, Joseph J., *His Excellency George Washington,* Alfred A. Knopf, 2004

McCullough, David, *1776,* Simon & Schuster, 2005.

McDonald, Forrest, *A Constitutional History of the United States,* Robert E. Krieger Publishing Company, 1986

Simon, James F., *What Kind of Nation: Thomas Jefferson, John Marshall, and the Epic Struggle to Create a United States,* Simon & Schuster, 2002.

Ferling, John, *Adams vs. Jefferson: The Tumultuous Election of 1800,* Oxford University Press, 2004

Larson, Edward J., *A Magnificent Catastrophe: The Tumultuous Election of 1800, America's First Presidential Campaign,* Free Press, 2007

Schweikart, Larry, and Allen, Michael, *A Patriot's History of the United States: From Columbus's Great Discovery to the War on Terror,* Sentinel, 2004

Sloan, Cliff and McKean, David, *The Great Decision: Jefferson, Adams, Marshall, and the Battle for the Supreme Court,* Public Affairs, 2009

# Economics

Booker, Christopher, *The Real Global Warming Disaster: Is the obsession with 'climate change' turning out to be the most costly scientific blunder in history?*, Continuum, 2009
Klein, Naomi, *The Shock Doctrine: The Rise of Disaster Capitalism*, Picador, 2007.

# "Problem" books

These are books that state the problems America faces because we have departed from the Constitution. Most of them offer very little in the way of practical solutions.

Bloom, Allan, *The Closing of the American Mind: How Higher Education Has Failed Democracy and Impoverished the Souls of Today's Students*, Simon and Schuster, 1987

Bork, Robert H., *Slouching Towards Gomorrah: Modern Liberalism and American Decline*, Reagan Books, HarperCollins, 1996

Flynn, Daniel J., *Why the Left hates America: Exposing the Lies That Have Obscured Our Nation's Greatness*, Forum, Prima Publishing, 2002

Gross, Martin L., *National Suicide: How Washington is Destroying the American Dream from A to Z*, Berkley Books, 2009. This is intended to be a "quick read".

Kick, Russ, editor, *You Are Being Lied To: the Disinformation Guide to Media Distortion, Historical Whitewashes and Cultural Myths*, The Disinformation Company Ltd., 2001. I don't like reading books like this, particularly when they offer no solutions. This oversized volume is not designed to be a "solution" book. It is an extensive discussion of numerous events in recent American history.

Levin, Mark, *Liberty and Tyranny: A Conservative Manifesto*, Threshold Editions, 2009. This book is meant to be a "quick read".

Ponnuru, Ramesh, *The Party of Death: The Democrats, the Media, the Courts, and the Disregard for Human Life,* Regnery Publishing, 2006

Schweizer, Peter, *Architects of Ruin: How Big Government Liberals Wrecked the Global Economy–and how they will do it again if no one stops them,* HarperCollins, 2009

Wiggin, Addison, and Bonner, Bill, *Empire of Debt: the Rise of an Epic Financial Crisis,* John Wiley & Sons, 2006.

Wiggin, Addison, and Incontrera, Kate, *I.O.U.S.A.: One Nation. Under Stress. In Debt,* John Wiley & Sons, 2008.

Wolf, Naomi, The End of America: Letter of Warning to a Young Patriot, Chelsea Green Publishing, 2007

# "Solution" Books

Brookhiser, Richard, What Would the Founders Do? (Our Questions / Their Answers), Basic Books, 2006

# Conservatism

Edwards, Mickey, Reclaiming Conservatism: How a Great American Political Movement Got Lost–and How It Can Find Its Way Back, Oxford University Press, 2008

# Democracy

Rahe, Paul A., Soft Despotism, Democracy's Drift: Montesquieu, Rousseau, Tocqueville, and the Modern Prospect, Yale University Press, 2009

De Tocqueville, Alexis, *Democracy in America,* Alfred A. Knopf, 1980 This is an important classic—and you'll be surprised to find that some of the things de Tocqueville is famous for saying were never said by him.

# Liberty

Bastiat, Frederic, *The Law*, The Foundation for Economic Education, Inc., 1968. This is a classic on free markets and natural law. It is a small but very important book.

# Political Correctness

Woods, Thomas E., Jr., *33 Questions about American History You're Not Supposed to Ask*, Crown Forum, 2007

# Socialism and Franklin Delano Roosevelt (FDR)

Folsom, Burton, Jr., *New Deal or Raw Deal: How FDR's Economic Legacy has Damaged America*, Threshold Editions, 2008

# Libertarian books

Libertarian books are different than books advocating a return to the Constitution. Libertarianism is in the often uncomfortable position of advocating for victimless crimes, which are deemed to include homosexuality, abortion, alcoholism, and drug abuse. The idea is that you can do whatever you want to yourself as long as it harms no one but yourself. This stand leaves Libertarians without an adequate moral foundation. I believe the Founding Fathers would have unanimously disapproved of Libertarianism. Even Congressman Ron Paul disagrees with the Party's stand on abortion.

Paul, Ron, *The Revolution; A Manifesto*, Grand Central Publishing, 2008

# Other Books Worth Reading

Diamond, Jared, *Collapse: How Societies Choose to Fail or Succeed*, Viking, 2005

Alinsky, Saul, *Rules for Radicals: A Pragmatic Primer for Realistic Radicals,* Vintage Books, 1989. This is the handbook used by Communists, Socialists, Democrats, liberals, leftists, and revolutionaries, including many in the American government today: why shouldn't we apply some of the same tactics, as long as they are not illegal, immoral, or unethical?

# Recommended Reading

The books in this list are recommended for all readers. The number indicates the order in which they may be read, beginning with the Constitution itself.

1. *The U.S. Constitution and Fascinating Facts About It,* Oak Hill Publishing Company, 2009. www.constitutionfacts.com . This is my favorite edition of the Constitution, and I have distributed many copies of it. Is worth the extra money it costs over the "free" versions.

Fineman, Howard, *The 13 American Arguments: Enduring Debates That Define and Inspire Our Country,* Random House, 2008

3. Hamilton, Alexander, Madison, James, and John Jay, *The Federalist Papers,* Bantam Books, 1982

6. McDonald, Forrest, *States' Rights and the Union: Imperium in Imperio, 1776–1876,* University press of Kansas, 2000. It's amazing how little we are taught in history class.

Padover, Saul K., *The Living U.S. Constitution,* Third Revised Edition, Meridian, 1995

Peters, William, *A More Perfect Union: The Making of the United States Constitution,* Crown Publishers, 1987. An excellent video is available from the National Center for Constitutional Studies.

2. Skousen, W. Cleon, *The Five Thousand Year Leap: The 28 Ideas That Changed the World,* National Center for Constitutional Studies 1981

# American History

Ellis, Joseph J., *Founding Brothers: The Revolutionary Generation*, Vintage Books, 2002. Joseph Ellis is an outstanding author. This is a history book, but its value to me is the insights it provides into the lives of some of the Founding Fathers.

Ellis, Joseph J., *His Excellency George Washington*, Alfred A. Knopf, 2004

4. McCullough, David, *1776*, Simon & Schuster, 2005. This is an absolutely wonderful book, particularly in the more recent edition which has pockets containing replicas of various documents from the period of 1776.

5. Simon, James F., *What Kind of Nation: Thomas Jefferson, John Marshall, and the Epic Struggle to Create a United States*, Simon & Schuster, 2002. Jefferson and Marshall fought tooth and nail over the power of the US Supreme Court; this book details how Jefferson lost every battle.

# Economics

Booker, Christopher, The *Real Global Warming Disaster: Is the obsession with 'climate change' turning out to be the most costly scientific blunder in history?*, Continuum, 2009

Klein, Naomi, *The Shock Doctrine: The Rise of Disaster Capitalism*, Picador, 2007. This book is a real eye-opener: I wish that everything Naomi Klein says about Milton Friedman and the effect of his teachings was wrong. This is one "economics" book you shouldn't shy away from; you will find a lot more readable and a lot more interesting than you might think.

# "Problem" books

Bork, Robert H., *Slouching Towards Gomorrah: Modern Liberalism and American Decline*, Reagan Books, HarperCollins, 1996

Gross, Martin L., *National Suicide: How Washington is Destroying the American Dream from A to Z*, Berkley Books, 2009. This is intended to be a "quick read".

Levin, Mark, *Liberty and Tyranny: A Conservative Manifesto*, Threshold Editions, 2009. This book is meant to be a "quick read".

Wiggin, Addison, and Bonner, Bill, *Empire of Debt: the Rise of an Epic Financial Crisis*, John Wiley & Sons, 2006. I recommend this book because it gives you some idea of how aggressive America has been in the past hundred and 50 years, and the price that all of us are now paying to sustain the "Empire of debt" that remains.

Wiggin, Addison, and Incontrera, Kate, *I.O.U.S.A.: One Nation. Under Stress. In Debt*, John Wiley & Sons, 2008. A DVD version of this book is available.

Wolf, Naomi, *The End of America: Letter of Warning to a Young Patriot*, Chelsea Green Publishing, 2007

## Liberty

7. Bastiat, Frederic, *The Law*, The Foundation for Economic Education, Inc., 1968. This is a classic on free markets and natural law. It is a small but very important book.

## Libertarian books

Libertarian books are different than books advocating a return to the Constitution. Libertarianism is in the often uncomfortable position of advocating for victimless crimes, which are deemed to include homosexuality, abortion, alcoholism, and drug abuse. The idea is that you can do whatever you want to yourself as long as it harms no one but yourself. This stand leaves Libertarians without an adequate moral foundation. I believe the Founding Fathers would have unanimously disapproved of Libertarianism. Even Congressman Ron Paul disagrees with the Party's stand on abortion.

Paul, Ron, *The Revolution; A Manifesto,* Grand Central Publishing, 2008

# Forms

The following forms are suggestions, and can be modified to meet local needs.

Forms include:

- Leadership Roster
- Talents and Abilities Survey
- Duties and Responsibilities of Committee Leaders

# Leadership Roster

_____ County Committee

Date: _____

| Position | Currently Serving | Date Installed | Proposed Replacement Candidate | Candidate Interview Date | Date Discussed with Council | Approved by Council (Yes/No) |
|---|---|---|---|---|---|---|
| *Committee Head | | | | | | |
| *Assistant Committee Head | | | | | | |
| *Treasurer | | | | | | |
| *Committee Secretary | | | | | | |
| *Committee Historian | | | | | | |
| *Activities Coordinator | | | | | | |

|  | | | | | |
|---|---|---|---|---|---|
| *Education Coordinator | | | | | |
| *Committee Website Editor | | | | | |
| *Trainer | | | | | |
| *Teacher, Continuing Education Class | | | | | |
| *Ballot Access Specialist | | | | | |
| Teacher, Basic Class | | | | | |
| Alternate Teacher | | | | | |
| Alternate Trainer | | | | | |
| Recruiter 1 | | | | | |
| Recruiter 2 | | | | | |
| Website Developer | | | | | |

(* indicates a member of the Executive Council)

# Talents and Abilities Survey

Name _____  Address _____

Phone # _____  City _____

Alternate Phone # _____  State, ZIP _____

Employer _____  Occupation _____

Education _____

Please circle your Talent (T), Interest (I), or Experience (E) in each
of the following areas, circling (N) when not applicable:

| | | | |
|---|---|---|---|
| 1. Public Speaking | T I E N | 2. Teaching | T I E N |
| 3. Leadership | T I E N | 4. Management | T I E N |
| 5. Website Development | T I E N | 6. Accounting | T I E N |
| 7. Database Management | T I E N | 8. Correspondence with elected officials | T I E N |
| 9. Bookkeeping | T I E N | 10. Political Activism | T I E N |
| 11. Interviewing | T I E N | 12. Training | T I E N |

Please comment on your responses for #s 1-12:

Item #                     Comments

_____

_____

_____

_____

_____

Where would you be most interested in serving in the Constitution Party?

_____

_____

# Duties and Responsibilities
## of Committee Leaders

| Position | Duties and Responsibilities | Suggested Term of Service |
|----------|------------------------------|----------------------------|
| * Committee Head | Leads the local Committee; heads the Executive Committee; shares the responsibility for conducting meetings with the Assistant Committee Head | 1 year |
| * Assistant Committee Head | Assists the Committee Leader; shares responsibility for conducting meetings; meets with the Executive Committee | 1 year |
| * Treasurer | Responsible for the collection and distribution of all Committee funds | 1 year |
| * Committee Secretary | Responsible for all correspondence except membership dues billings | 1 year |

| Position | Duties and Responsibilities | Suggested Term of Service |
|---|---|---|
| * Committee Historian | Responsible for preparing meeting agendas, maintaining attendance rolls, taking minutes at meetings | 1 year |
| * Activities Coordinator | Identifies appropriate events for political activism and, in conjunction with the Executive Committee, arranges for Party participation | 1 year |
| * Education Coordinator | Works with local school districts and PTAs, universities, and colleges to have the Constitution and the principles of freedom taught regularly in each setting. | 1 year |
| * Committee Website Editor | Creates and updates all materials posted on the Committee website | 1 year |
| * Trainer | Provides training at Committee meetings and at events, as appropriate | 1 year |

| Position | Duties and Responsibilities | Suggested Term of Service |
| --- | --- | --- |
| * Teacher, Continuing Education Class | Teaches the expanded Constitution class, with focus on current issues and appropriate Constitutional solutions. Coordinates use of materials from the National Committee | 3-6 months |
| * Ballot Access Specialist | Obtains ballot access for all local CP candidates | 1 year |
| Teacher, Basic Class | Teaches the basic Constitution class using appropriate materials provided by the National Committee, the NCCS, and other sources | 3-6 months |
| Alternate Teacher | Teaches as a substitute or on a rotating basis either the Basic Class or the Continuing Education Class | 3-6 months |
| Alternate Trainer | Provides training as a substitute or on a rotating basis at Committee meetings and events | 1 year |

| Position | Duties and Responsibilities | Suggested Term of Service |
|----------|----------------------------|---------------------------|
| Recruiter 1 | Conducts interviews or prospective Party members, prospective Party leaders, and prospective CP candidates for public office | 1 year |
| Recruiter 2 | Conducts interviews or prospective Party members, prospective Party leaders, and prospective CP candidates for public office | 1 year |
| Website Developer | Creates and maintains the Committee website | 1 year |

(* indicates a member of the Executive Council)

# Endnotes

1  This statement was made by then-US Senator Barack Hussein Obama in 2008 as he was campaigning for the Presidency of the United States. The author heard him make the statement, but has not been able to locate a recording of the event.

2  Thanks to Herman Cain for his talk about S-I-N at CPAC 2010.

3  Nacht und Nebel was a secret order issued by Adolf Hitler on December 7, 1941, under which "persons endangering German security" in the German-occupied territories of western Europe were to be arrested and either shot or spirited away under cover of "night and fog" (that is, clandestinely) to concentration camps. (Source: *Encyclopedia Britannica*, Multimedia edition 2009)

4  *Choosing Federalism, Choosing Freedom*, article by Timothy Baldwin, 2009, http://libertydefenseleague.com

5  *States' Rights and the Union: Imperium in Imperio*, 1776–1876, Forrest McDonald, University of Kansas press, 2000, pp. 8–9. Most of this lengthy quote is taken *from To Make a Nation: The Rediscovery of American Federalism* by Samuel H. Beer, Cambridge, Mass, 1993, and from *A Necessary Evil: A History of American Distrust of Government*, Garry Wills, New York, 1999.

6  Ibid., page 9. This is a quote from *The Continental Congress*, Edmund Cody Burnet, New York, 1941.

7   *National Suicide: How Washington is destroying the American dream from A-Z,* Martin L. Gross, Berkley books, New York, 2009, pp. 305–307.

8   The Declaration of Independence, paragraph 2.

9   Tyler Cowan, as quoted by Sheldon Richmond, *Corruption in Government? Shocking!*

Other books by Charles Kraut:

*Moneywise: Your Guide to Keeping Ahead of Inflation, Taxes, and the Declining Dollar*